BRAVE GIRLS
Better Than Perfect

Other books in the Brave Girls brand

Brave Girls Bible Stories

Brave Girls: Faithful Friends

BRAVE GIRLS
Better Than Perfect

Written by
JENNIFER GERELDS

A Division of Thomas Nelson Publishers

NASHVILLE   MEXICO CITY   RIO DE JANEIRO

Published in Nashville, Tennessee, by Tommy Nelson. Tommy Nelson is an imprint of Thomas Nelson. Thomas Nelson is a registered trademark of HarperCollins Christian Publishing, Inc.

Thomas Nelson titles may be purchased in bulk for educational, business, fund-raising, or sales promotional use. For information, please e-mail SpecialMarkets@ThomasNelson.com.

Unless otherwise noted, Scripture quotations are taken from International Children's Bible®. © 1986, 1988, 1999 by Thomas Nelson, Inc. All rights reserved.

Scripture quotations marked NKJV are taken from The New King James Version. © 1982 by Thomas Nelson, Inc. Used by permission. All rights reserved.

Library of Congress Cataloging-in-Publication Data is on file.

Printed in the United States of America

15 16 17 18 19 20 QG 6 5 4 3 2 1

Contents

Introduction

> God began doing a good work in you. And
> He will continue it until it is finished when
> Jesus Christ comes again. I am sure of that.
>
> Philippians 1:6

Faith and I (Honor) were hanging out the other day. We had some time to kill because we had just finished writing this book on self-esteem, so we decided to work on a puzzle together. I couldn't wait to finish it because the final picture was going to be of these really cute koalas, some of my favorite animals.

But it took a lot longer than I expected. It was difficult making the pieces fit. They didn't look anything like the finished picture when they first came out of the box! But slowly, as it came together piece by piece, the picture got clearer.

And then it dawned on both of us: that puzzle is exactly like our lives! God created each one of us as a wonderfully unique and beautiful picture of Him. When He looks at us, He sees the finished picture—like the cover on the puzzle box. We, however, only see the little puzzle pieces of our lives. To be honest, some of those pieces don't look very nice, and it's really tough to see how they could ever fit into God's plan to make something beautiful.

Yeah, but that's where faith comes in! (Not me, of course. I mean actual trust in God!) We might not understand why God gave us the family—or the nose or eye color or life circumstances—that He did. To us, it might even look like a mess, which can make a perfectionist like me feel nervous . . . until I remember the bigger picture. God has already made me perfect in Jesus! And God uses all of life's events to put the pieces in place, making a beautiful work of art in the end.

So we've written this book to help you see what God sees: perfection in process. We want you to know how much God loves you and thinks you're wonderful—and how much we all need Him to help us be the people He created us to be. When you're finished reading, we hope you'll celebrate God's creativity and goodness in you. God is good! And it's good to see Him in you!

Love,

Honor & Faith

Honor
Faith

TRUTH DETECTIVES

CHildReN, obey youR paReNts iN all
tHiNgs. THis pleases tHe LoRd.

Colossians 3:20

Lie: I Need to get my owN way to be Happy.

You know the feeling: you want to spend the night with your friend *so* badly. Or you want that candy you saw in the checkout line. Or you just want to watch the TV show that *all* your friends get to watch. But instead, you hear the word *no* coming from your parents.

Immediately, you want to argue. "But why?" you begin. Then your brain starts churning like a train—slowly at first and then gaining speed. "But everybody's going" or "You never buy me anything" or "There's nothing wrong with it." With every word, you hope to convince your parents they're wrong.

The TRutH Is . . .

Why do you put up such a fight to get what you want? It's likely you've been duped by the lie "I need to get my own way to be happy."

Actually, you'll feel—and live—better when you trust and obey God's ways, even though you really think you want something else. (Remember Adam and Eve when they chose their own way instead of God's?) Listening to and obeying your parents will put you on the path to greater happiness.

The next time you hear the word *no* from your parents, stop and thank God for giving you leaders who love you and want the best for you. Then ask Him to help you obey Him with a happy heart. You'll be glad you did!

PRayeR PoiNteR

Father, help me obey my parents so I can live better.

> THe LORD laughs at those who
> laugh at Him. But He is kind to
> those who are not proud.
>
> PROVERbs 3:34

Lie: I always need to be right.

"That's not how you do it," Maggie told her friend Chloe as she was drawing a picture.

"Well, I like it like it is," Chloe said without looking up.

"Look," Maggie answered, taking the pencil and paper out of Chloe's hands. "If you change it like this, it looks better," she reasoned as she started to erase Chloe's picture.

"Leave my paper alone," Chloe mumbled as she took her things back and moved to another table.

The Truth Is . . .

It definitely feels good when we think we're right. The problem with needing to be right all the time is that we are only thinking about ourselves and how smart we think we are. But our egos keep us from considering other people's needs. Just because something may be true doesn't mean it needs to be said. For instance, comments like "You're fat" or "You don't have any friends" may actually be true statements, but that information is *not* helpful.

Instead of being right, being kind would be a much better

option. In Maggie's case, a word of encouragement would have bonded their friendship a lot better than a word of correction. But when the moment does call for speaking the truth, make sure it is spoken in love. Because love, not being right, always wins.

Prayer Pointer

Lord, You hate pride but love the humble. Help
me humbly love the others around me.

Brand-New Style

Day 3

> [The LORD] has covered me with
> a coat of goodness.
>
> Isaiah 61:10

Lie: I need to wear the latest brands and styles.

"Mom, I need a new backpack," Emma said.

"Why? We just got you a new backpack a month ago," her mom countered.

"Yeah, but I need the same backpack as the other girls."

"You mean the $100 kind?"

"Um, yeah," Emma huffed. "I don't want to be, like, a nerd or anything."

The Truth Is . . .

God says that true worth comes from your connections. Unfortunately, a lot of girls think that if they are connected to the popular kids at school, then they will have a better self-image and life.

But girls were created for a far more important connection: one with God. When you know that God thinks you're awesome and stays by your side no matter what, well, suddenly the drive for the latest fashion starts to lose some steam. We don't have to build our self-esteem based on opinions of other people. Instead, we need to stand on the promise of God's lasting favor and show the world a better way to live.

Prayer Pointer

Lord, help me believe You love me and shut
out the pressure to be like everyone else.

6

Busy Bodies

God says, "Be quiet and know that I am God."

Psalm 46:10

Lie: I need to be busy.

"So, are you going out for the soccer team?" Kate asked.

"N-not sure," Lizzy stammered. "I mean, I haven't decided."

"How about the drama group, then? Or choir?"

"Probably not."

"Wow. I guess you just like being boring," Kate concluded.

The Truth Is . . .

People today *are* very busy. Just ask anyone. They can list any number of activities, sports, and projects they are doing. And a lot of it might sound pretty important. But are people *too* busy? God says that He wants us to be still and know that He is God. When we can barely catch our breath from our activities, we are missing what is most important: time for our friendship with God.

So why do we stay so busy? Maybe because everyone else seems to be doing it. Maybe quiet time makes us nervous. Maybe we feel more important if we are accomplishing a lot of things. But we need to remember what Jesus told His busy friend, Martha, in Luke 10: more important than filling our time with activities is filling it with Him.

Prayer Pointer

Lord, help me make time for You by saying
no to activities I don't need in my life.

7

"WHEN you aRe weak, tHEN my poweR
is made peRfect iN you." So I am veRy
Happy to bRag about my weakNesses.
THEN CHRist's poweR caN live iN me.

2 CoRiNtHiaNs 12:9

Lie: I Have to be smaRt to Have value.

Sarah was in a panic as she held her returned test paper marked with a giant D at the top. "Oh no!" she gasped. "My parents are going to kill me." Then her mind began to race: *I'll probably flunk out of fourth grade. I don't know how I'll ever make it to middle school or high school. Probably shouldn't even think about college. I'm just an idiot, and that's all I'm ever going to be.*

THe TRutH Is . . .

It can be really frustrating when it seems like everyone is smarter than you. Teachers and even well-meaning parents can add to the pressure by trying to help you succeed. But do you want to know another secret truth? God—you know, the One who created your brain—has a plan for your life.

More important than landing an A is learning how to trust God with our weaknesses and believing that He is able to take

us wherever we need to go, regardless of our seeming limitations. Remember, you are friends with an awesome God, and He promises to take care of you. So stop beating yourself up, and thank God for making you like He did. Ask Him to help you do your best while depending on Him to take care of the rest.

Prayer Pointer

Lord, the smartest thing I can do is trust
You. Thank You for taking care of me.

We all have different gifts.
Each gift came because of the
grace that God gave us.

Romans 12:6

Lie: I need to have a better personality.

"I wish I were like her," Hannah admitted to her friend Avery.

Both girls watched Lexi, the new girl, who seemed to have the entire class wrapped around her finger. From where they stood, they could see she was the center of attention amid the group of popular kids, laughing and smiling and carrying on like conversation with those kids was the most natural thing in the world.

"Yeah, she's just so outgoing and funny," Avery agreed.

The Truth Is . . .

Now try to imagine if everyone in the world were like Lexi. Sure, everybody would love to talk and entertain, but who would be listening? How would any work ever get done? While some personalities seem to sparkle and shine more than others, God actually designed each kind for His purposes—and most of His work doesn't require center stage.

Are you quiet or shy? Are you determined and focused? Are you bold and aggressive? No matter what kind of personality God has

mixed into your character, you can be sure that God will use it for His glory if you give your life to Him. Just ask Him to use little ol' you in the spotlight or behind the scenes to shine out His glory like only you can do.

Prayer Pointer

Lord, I'm here to glorify You, not me. Please
use me to help others see You.

Your teachings are worth more to me than
thousands of pieces of gold and silver.

Psalm 119:72

Lie: I need to have money to be happy.

"Mom, Casey's family is flying to Colorado to go skiing this spring break," said Hadley.

"Hmm, that's nice," Mom answered.

"Mom?" asked Hadley. "Why don't we ever go skiing for spring break?"

"Well, hon, we have a pretty big family, and we don't have that kind of money. Plus, we can find fun things to do around here, can't we?"

"I guess," Hadley moped. To herself she muttered, "But sometimes I wish I lived in Casey's family."

The Truth Is . . .

God not only meets our needs—He's what we need most! While some people have more money and more things than other people, real joy does not come with a price tag that only the wealthy can afford. God has given us the ticket to peace and joy when we choose to thank Him for His presence in our lives and trust His promise to meet our needs. Being content with what God has given us allows us to think about how we can help other people instead

of strategizing how to get more for ourselves. Jesus Himself said that it is better to give than to receive (Acts 20:35). When we give, we grow rich—not necessarily with money but with the experience of God's love. Living by God's economy, we find that we never run out of what we need most: Him.

Prayer Pointer

Father, I need You more than anything in the world. Thank You for providing for me!

> CHaRm caN fool you, aNd beauty caN tRick you. But a womaN wHo Respects tHe LORD sHould be pRaised.
>
> PRoveRbs 31:30

Lie: I Need to be beautiful.

Jess had already been in the bathroom staring at the mirror for over half an hour. No matter how she styled her hair, she just didn't think it looked pretty.

"Ugh!" she grunted in frustration. "My hair looks awful! My face looks awful! Why am I so ugly?"

THe TRutH Is . . .

Have you ever heard that beauty is in the eye of the beholder? It's an old phrase that means beauty is determined more by the person looking at it and appreciating it rather than the object itself. The truth is that different things seem beautiful to different people.

So what kind of beautiful do you want to be? If you're a child of God, the most important person beholding your beauty is your heavenly Father. He planned your nose and your hair, your freckles and your height before He even formed the planet! He put a lot of thought into you and made you in the perfect way that makes Him smile with delight. You are gorgeous in His eyes no matter what you think the mirror says! So forget the cover of that magazine or what makes the girls at school *oooh* and *ahhh*. The secret to being beautiful is seeing yourself through God's eyes.

―――――― PRayeR PoiNteR ――――――

Lord, help me see myself the way You see me: beautiful.

The Best Loser

Everything you say and everything you do should all be done for Jesus your Lord.

Colossians 3:17

Lie: I need to win to feel good about myself.

"Let's play one more round," Livvy insisted.

"Nooooo," Marlie moaned as she rolled onto her back. "We've played this game, like, three times now!"

"I know, but it isn't fair," Livvy said, growing irritated. "You always get the good cards, so we have to play until I can win."

The Truth Is . . .

While some people are more competitive than others, it's not fun for anybody to lose. And yet someone has to lose in order for someone to win, right? And since it isn't likely—or even fair—that you will always win, then it's just as important to learn to lose well.

Losing well means not having a temper tantrum, accusing others of cheating, or having a bad attitude. It also means being glad for others and grateful for the chance to play at all. Remember, winning doesn't make you a better person. But winning or losing with a good attitude makes you the kind of person other people like to play with.

Prayer Pointer

Lord, help me win, lose, and play in a
way that shows Your grace.

There is a right time for everything.
Everything on earth has its special season.

Ecclesiastes 3:1

Lie: I need to be on top of the latest technology trends.

"Mom, I need you to help me set up a Web account," Camryn said.

"An account on what site?" her mom queried.

"It's not a big deal. I just want to post some pictures."

"Aren't you a little young for that?" her mom responded, growing concerned.

"No, all my friends are doing it."

Her mom frowned. "That may be what everybody else is doing, but I don't think it's wise for you—not at this age, anyway."

The Truth Is . . .

Timing is important. Unfortunately, learning to wait for the things we want right now can be really difficult, especially when our friends or older siblings *aren't* having to wait for it. So many social media sites look like fun with pictures of all the great things it seems like everybody (but you) is doing. But age restrictions on those sites exist for a reason. And your mom, despite her possible lack of tech know-how, *does* know a thing or two about staying safe on the Internet.

Instead of rushing to be like everyone else, learn self-control, and try building relationships face-to-face instead. As you grow in God and learn how to relate well to others in real life, you will be better equipped when the right time comes to handle the perks and problems of online life.

PRayeR PoiNteR

Lord, help me to be patient and trust that You've
given my parents the wisdom to guide me.

If I wanted to please men, I would
not be a servant of Christ.

Galatians 1:10

Lie: I need for everyone to like me.

Erika's stomach hurt with the stress of it all. Jessica and some other girls wanted her to join them on the soccer team. But Erika knew God had gifted her better at dance. *If I choose dance instead of soccer, all those girls are going to get mad and ignore me*, Erika reasoned. *And I don't want to have to deal with that all year.*

The next day Erika told her mom she was going out for the soccer team. "It's just easier that way," she concluded.

The Truth Is . . .

We really only need to please one person, and you won't find Him in your yearbook. God says that the only one worth working hard to please is Himself! The great news is that He is already pleased with you. So all that pressure you feel when you try to make everybody happy can slide right off your shoulders.

God hasn't given you the impossible task of making everyone like you. But He *has* asked you to follow Him, paying careful attention to His voice and doing what He has called you to do.

When you seek to please God instead of people, your happiness and sense of purpose will grow deeper in God, no matter what others may do or say.

Prayer Pointer

Lord, I want to please You with all I say and do. Help me keep my focus on You and not my friends.

Do all you can to live a peaceful life. Take
care of your own business. Do your own work.

1 Thessalonians 4:12

Lie: I need to have fun all the time.

"Mom, I'm bored," Lindsey muttered. "What are we going to do today?"

"Well," answered her mother, "I have a mountain of laundry to tackle, and then I was going to take a meal for that lady in our church who had surgery. Want to help me with that?"

"That's not fun," Lindsey moaned as she walked out of the room.

The Truth Is . . .

Work is not a result of sin in the world, but our bad attitude about it is. Even in the garden of Eden before the fall, Adam had to name the animals and tend to the garden (Genesis 2:15, 19–20). Work is a part of what God created us to do. But when we let our own selfish desires take over, doing work—from homework to yard work to community service and more—seems like a chore. Add to that all the entertainment options around us, from shopping to movies to computers, and we actually begin to believe we deserve to be entertained every moment of the day.

But the truth is that life as a child of God involves both work and play, all to be carried out with an attitude of thankfulness and

joy. So has your dad asked you to weed the yard? Help with a happy heart. Has your friend invited you to a round of mini-golf? Swing away with gratefulness. Bored? Look around you to see how you can be of service. In working hard, you serve God, bless others, and discover a whole new level of fun and reward.

Prayer Pointer

Lord, help me stop looking for entertainment
and start finding ways to bless others.

"Your giving should be done in secret.
Your Father can see what is done in
secret, and He will reward you."

Matthew 6:4

Lie: I need to be noticed and appreciated.

"Notice anything different?" Taylor asked her sister, Alyssa.

"No, what?" Alyssa answered, clueless.

In a huff, Taylor blurted, "Your toys! I straightened all your mess!"

Then Taylor marched upstairs to her mom. "Mom, no one ever appreciates all the work I do around here," she complained.

Her mom answered gently, "I know how you feel, Taylor. But there is Someone who always sees the good we do," she reminded her. "He's who we work for anyway, right?"

The Truth Is . . .

Taylor's mom hit right at the heart of Taylor's problem. Taylor was doing a very good work by serving her sister, but the kindness was lost when she demanded attention and looked for thanks. Jesus wants us to follow His example instead. He certainly stayed busy serving the disciples and the crowds who followed Him, but His

motive was not to receive glory for Himself (though He was actually worthy). Everything He did was to point people to the Father.

Our service needs to be the same. When we love and serve secretly, we get the joy of blessing others in a way that God alone gets the credit. Yet we also know that our heavenly Father is watching us and has promised to reward us for the secret good we do.

Prayer Pointer

Lord, I want to point people to how good You are, not to me. Help me serve in secret.

> You are living with crooked and mean
> people all around you. Among them you
> shine like stars in the dark world.
>
> Philippians 2:15

Lie: I need to be famous.

Mandy was watching her favorite singing competition show on TV. It was down to the final two contestants.

"I would give anything to be on stage like that," she mused out loud to her brother. "Wouldn't it be awesome to have everybody know your name and think you're really talented?"

"It'd probably be pretty fun for a while," he agreed.

"Yeah, and everywhere you went, people would know you, and you could get whatever you wanted."

"True, but fame does seem to have its drawbacks," he answered thoughtfully.

The Truth Is . . .

It seems like everyone is clamoring to become the next superstar sensation. But why? What is at the heart of wanting to become famous? The truth is that we all have a fear deep inside that we are not special. We think we are just one of billions of people on this planet who doesn't do anything to give our short time on this earth

any particular meaning. So we figure if we can get a great career or become a famous performer or politician, we will stand out. People will notice us. We will matter.

But God tells you, child of God, that you *do* matter because He sees you (out of all the billions of people) and loves *you*. And because His Spirit lives in you, you already shine like a star in a dark universe. Even if the people around you can't see it now, all of heaven does.

Don't get stuck in the vain search for fame. Instead, work hard to make God, your Father, known.

Prayer Pointer

Lord, I want my life to reflect how brilliant
You are. Thanks for loving me!

The Perfect Lie

Surely there is not a good man on earth who always does good and never sins.

Ecclesiastes 7:20

Lie: I can never make mistakes.

"That's what I meant to do," Sarah lied to her sister, Alli.

"Sure, you meant to fall on your bottom," Alli said, giggling.

"Quit making fun of me," Sarah growled as she stormed out of the kitchen.

"Why can't you ever loosen up?" Alli called after her. "I mean, it's like you can't ever admit when you've messed up! You're not perfect, you know!"

The Truth Is . . .

As much as it might bother Sarah to admit it, Alli is right. Sarah is not perfect, and neither is anyone else. The harder we try to always appear right and without fault, the more miserable we will be. Pretending to be perfect is exhausting!

Instead, God wants us to be humble, understanding that we are all sinners who say and do the wrong things at times and that we all need help. Fortunately, Jesus loves to help the humble in heart. So when you mess up, quit the cover-up. Confess it and smile. God's grace is much greater than your goof-ups, and His love knows no end.

Prayer Pointer

Thank You, Lord, that Your perfection is
good enough to cover all my failures.

Write It Out

What lies have you been telling yourself?
How can you replace them with God's truths?

_____

_____

_____

_____

_____

_____

_____

_____

_____

_____

_____

BIBLE BEAUTIES AND BEAUS

Eve

The First in Beauty and Grace

We were spiritually dead because of the things we did wrong against God. But God gave us new life with Christ. You have been saved by God's grace.

Ephesians 2:5

At first sight, Adam was amazed by Eve—God's answer to Adam's deep need for a companion equal to himself. When God realized what Adam was lacking, He made Eve from Adam's own rib. (Fortunately, God put Adam to sleep first!)

Eve was the first woman, the beginning of a beautiful work that would continue through the ages. Sadly, Eve's reign as the queen of Eden ended when she chose to disobey God's instructions, listening to the crafty snake (Satan) instead. Adam joined her, and both became separated from God because of their sin. God, however, loved His people too much to end the story there. God promised to send a Savior who could erase their sins and reunite them with God. (Read the whole story in Genesis 2–3.) Many years later, Jesus came and fulfilled God's promise (1 John 3:8). Because of God, Eve would no longer be known only as the first beautiful woman who sinned. Now she was also known as the first woman to know God's saving grace.

Prayer Pointer

Lord, thank You for Your beautiful grace and forgiveness.

Noah

The One Who Stood Alone

"The gate that opens the way to true life is very small. And the road to true life is very hard. Only a few people find that road."

Matthew 7:14

If everybody in your class started talking because the teacher left the room, would you stay quiet and work? If your siblings decided to sneak food into their bedrooms (even though Mom's rule is food at the kitchen table only), would you disobey too? When lots of people make the same wrong choice, it starts to seem okay, which makes it even more difficult to stand for what's right.

Just ask Noah. Everybody around him was choosing to disobey God, yet Noah kept his eyes on God. He listened to what God said and obeyed Him, even though everybody else probably thought he was crazy for building a boat in the desert.

Noah and his family were the only people who survived the great flood God sent to wipe out the evil in the world. Even though the story is a little scary (you can read all about it in Genesis 6–9), it is a great reminder of how important it is to stick with God instead of the world. In the big ways (like building a boat in the desert) or small ways (working quietly or choosing to honor Mom), following God brings the biggest blessing—to yourself and those around you.

Prayer Pointer

Father, help me hear Your voice and
follow You instead of the world.

Abraham

The Believer

ABRaHam believed God, and God accepted
ABRaHam's faitH, and tHat faitH made Him RigHt
witH God. And ABRaHam was called "God's fRiend."

James 2:23

When God told Abram to go to a new land, Abram packed up his bags and moved. When God told him that he would have more descendants than stars in the sky, Abram believed it—and God changed his name to Abraham, which means "the father of many." When God said he would have a son, Abraham watched and waited, though it took a long time. And when God asked him to sacrifice Isaac, that beloved son, Abraham obeyed until God stopped him at the last second (Genesis 12; 17; 21–22 for Abraham's amazing story).

So what makes Abraham so remarkable? Abraham believed that God was going to keep every promise He made. Abraham's amazing story reminds us that the key to pleasing God lies not in what we can do for God, but in believing who God is and trusting what He says.

So what about you? Do you trust that God has a plan for you and that it's every bit as good as what He promised Abraham? Then tell God so, and sense His smile. You are walking in Father Abraham's footsteps of faith.

PRayeR PointeR

Father, I believe that You are faithful to keep all Your
promises. Thank You for loving me so much!

The Lady in Waiting

Be strong and brave and wait for the Lord's help.

Psalm 27:14

Sarah handled moving from home like a champ. She even trusted God to take care of her when Abraham told her to follow some dangerously risky instructions. But waiting for a baby? Sarah wasn't sure she could make it. The years passed, and she still didn't have a baby to hold. So she panicked and had her maidservant, Hagar, bear a child with Abraham for her. But that wasn't God's way of answering His promise.

While Sarah waited, she grew old—like gray-hair-and-rocking-chair old. But one day God sent a messenger to tell her she was going to have a baby! The wrinkles on her face creased into a smile, then a laugh. *How could a woman my age have a baby?* she thought. But in less than a year, Sarah had Isaac, the long-awaited baby boy (Genesis 21:1–7).

Sarah's story shows us the beauty of waiting on God—and the problems that come when we don't. Worrying or trying to make things happen the way we want them to only frustrates us and keeps us from watching God work miracles. When we learn to wait patiently for God to meet our needs, we learn to trust that He will make good on His promise.

Prayer Pointer

Lord, help me to be patient and wait
for You to lead me and use me.

Hagar

The One Who Was Seen

"Yes, God even knows how many
hairs you have on your head. Don't
be afraid. You are worth much
more than many sparrows."

Luke 12:7

Have you ever felt forgotten, like no one really cares about you? Being lonely can make us feel scared. But sometimes God takes us to those lonely places so that we see He's with us.

Just ask Hagar, Sarah's servant who was forced to bear a child because Sarah couldn't have one. But when God gave Sarah the son she had always wanted, Sarah told Abraham to send Hagar and her boy away. So Hagar was cast out of the family. Wandering in the desert with her son, Hagar figured she was all alone and would die that way.

But God saw her. In fact, He saved them, showing them where to find fresh water and how to live (Genesis 21:9–20).

Hagar's story is a beautiful reminder that no matter where you go or what you do, God sees, cares, and is with you. He alone is powerful to save and walk with you all the days of your life.

Prayer Pointer

Lord, because of Your love, I am never alone. Thank
You for being my Savior and Friend forever.

Rebekah

The Risk Taker

THe LoRd GOD Helps me. So I will NoT be asHamed. I
will be deTeRmiNed. I kNow I will NoT be disgRaced.

IsaiaH 50:7

Young Rebekah was just drawing water for her sheep like she
did every day when she saw an unfamiliar man by the well.
Suddenly, she had the strong feeling she should give water
to all his camels. So she did. (Little did she know the stranger was
praying to God at that moment for the right woman to water his
camels.) When she finished, the man rewarded her with beautiful
gold jewelry and told her he believed God had chosen her to marry
the man's master, Isaac.

"Are you willing to leave your family and follow me back to my
master to marry Isaac?" the servant wanted to know.

"Yes!" Rebekah decided. Even though it was a scary leap of faith,
she knew God had an exciting adventure ahead for her if she simply obeyed and followed God's plan. Rebekah took the risk because
she and her family trusted God and believed that He never fails His
people. (See Genesis 24:12–58 for the whole story.)

What has God asked you to do today?

PRayeR PoiNteR

Lord, Your way is always right. Please
help me trust and follow You.

The One Who Felt Unloved

I praise you because you made me in
an amazing and wonderful way.

Psalm 139:14

Leah probably always knew her younger sister was prettier than she was. When Jacob first came to their land, it was Rachel who caught his attention and won his love. But after Jacob worked for seven years to marry Rachel, Leah and Rachel's father tricked Jacob into marrying Leah instead. This made Jacob upset, of course, so he worked another seven years to marry Rachel. All of her life, Leah probably knew she wasn't the prettiest or the most wanted in the group. Yet God loved her. He chose her to be the mother of many sons who grew to become the first leaders of Israel. He had great plans for Leah that were far more important than how she looked on the outside. (Read about Leah in Genesis 30:16–35).

Maybe you can relate to Leah. Sometimes kids can be mean and leave us out of the group or make us feel unimportant. And if we believe other people look better than we do, we can feel bad about ourselves. But Leah's story lets us know that no matter what, you are a treasure in God's eyes, and He has promised you a future full of hope and His never-ending love.

Prayer Pointer

Father, Your love for me means that I am special.
Thank You for making me the way You did.

Joseph

The One Who Forgave

Forgive each other because the Lord forgave you.

Colossians 3:13

Have your siblings ever done something mean to you? Maybe they broke your favorite toy or called you a bad name. When the people closest to us hurt us, the pain can be very deep and difficult to heal.

Imagine how Joseph must have felt. One day he went out to the field where his brothers were tending sheep to check on them, and they threw him in a dry well. Some even wanted to kill him. The brothers finally decided to sell Joseph to Egyptian traders. In Egypt, Joseph was put in prison, even though he did nothing wrong.

But Joseph knew God was in control and loved him. Years later, when Joseph was put in charge of Egypt's food, his brothers came to him because they and their families were starving. Instead of being angry, Joseph said, "You meant to do evil to me, but God meant it for good." (Read the whole story in Genesis 37–45.)

No matter what happens, we know that God has promised to work everything for our good. God gives us the power we need to forgive others and keep a loving attitude toward everyone God puts in our lives.

Prayer Pointer

Jesus, help me forgive others the way
that You have forgiven me.

The Girl Who Helped

Respect the LORD your God. Serve only Him.

Deuteronomy 6:13

Times were tough. The new Pharaoh had ordered that all the Israelites' baby boys be killed. But Jochebed and Amram didn't obey orders when their baby Moses was born. Instead, Jochebed nursed Moses until he was too old to hide and then crafted a floating basket to place him in the river near Egypt's palace.

Miriam, Moses' older sister, watched the floating basket until it was discovered by Pharaoh's daughter, who was bathing nearby. When the princess saw it, she had her attendants retrieve the basket. She wanted to keep the baby, but how would she take care of him?

"I'll find a Hebrew woman who could nurse him for you," Miriam volunteered boldly. The princess happily agreed to Miriam's idea! So Miriam got their mom to take care of Moses until he was old enough to be in Pharaoh's courts (Exodus 2:1–10).

Do you like to help your family? Taking in the groceries or vacuuming might not seem as glamorous as Miriam's amazing role, but every part we play in helping God's people *is* important. It shapes our character to be like Jesus, and God uses our acts of kindness to grow His kingdom, one helping deed at a time.

Prayer Pointer

Lord, help me see the needs around me
and be quick to help whenever I can.

The One Who Spoke for God

"Say the things God gives you to say at that time. It will not really be you speaking. It will be the Holy Spirit."

Mark 13:11

D o you like to talk in front of crowds? Moses didn't. But as he met with God in the burning bush, God gave Moses a clear command: "Go back to Egypt and tell Pharaoh to let My people go."

Gulp. Moses didn't want to go back to the place where he was hated. (He had killed an Egyptian years ago, and Pharaoh wanted him dead.) He especially didn't want to stand in front of Pharaoh to demand the Hebrews' freedom.

Yet that's what God wanted Moses to do. And God assured Moses that He would help him in his weakness. He even allowed Aaron, Moses' brother, to come alongside and speak for him. And God used them both to defeat Pharaoh and free His people in the most spectacular way imaginable at the Red Sea. (You can read about Moses in Exodus 3–14.)

So what do you think are your greatest weaknesses? Remember Moses' story, and realize that the God who helped Moses helps you too. You have everything you need to obey and succeed in doing whatever God calls you to do.

Prayer Pointer

Father, when I am weak, You are strong.
Give me the strength to obey You.

The Two Who Saw God's Greatness

My dear children, you belong to God. So you have defeated them because God's Spirit, who is in you, is greater than the devil, who is in the world.

1 John 4:4

Moses sent twelve spies to look at the land God had promised to give His people. Each spy came back agreeing that the land was amazing and filled with all the good things God had promised. But ten of the twelve said it also had scary-looking giants living there. They didn't think God was big enough to handle such intimidating warriors.

But Joshua and Caleb, the other two spies, saw the situation quite differently. They remembered how great God had been in providing for His people, and they believed God would keep His goodness going. As a result, only Joshua and Caleb were allowed by God to enter the promised land when the time came (Numbers 13–14:9, 30).

Do you have any giants in your life? Not the tall-people kind, but situations in your family or at school or church that just seem too big for you to handle? Turn to God like Joshua and Caleb did, and think about all the ways God has helped you in the past. He is faithful to help you conquer your fears as He strengthens and guides you all the way.

Prayer Pointer

Lord, nothing is too difficult for You to handle.
You are my Protector and Provider!

Rahab

The One Who Started Over

As for me and my family, we will serve the LORD.

Joshua 24:15

Rahab was supposed to be one of Israel's enemies. Born and raised in Jericho, she had done many of the evil deeds that had made God angry at the nation. But when she heard about God, she wanted to change sides.

So when Israel sent spies into Jericho, she hid them in her home. Then she helped them escape in exchange for her family's safety when Israel came to attack the city. Because Rahab chose to side with God and His people, only she and her family survived when God collapsed Jericho's walls and Israel's soldiers destroyed every living thing in the city. Best of all, Rahab was accepted into the Hebrew family and married one of the spies who had come to visit that fateful night (Joshua 2; 6:22–25).

Sometimes we can find ourselves in a situation like Rahab's. We realize we have been living a life that displeases God. But Rahab's story gives us great hope! God always receives us when we turn to Him for help. So confess your bad choices to God, and ask Him to help you become the person He wants you to be. God is always happy to welcome a new member into the family!

Prayer Pointer

Father, please forgive my sin of _____.
Save me, and make me Your own.

41

David

The Boy with a Great God

THe LORD youR God fighTs foR you, as
He pRomised to do. So you must be
caReful to love tHe LORD youR God.

JosHua 23:10-11

They all took one look at David and moaned, "He's just a boy! Goliath is a strong and powerful soldier!"

From all appearances, it didn't look like David the shepherd boy was the right choice to go up against the great Philistine warrior, and much was at stake. The winner of the fight would win the entire war. The loser would make his nation slaves to the victor. But weeks had passed, and though the giant Goliath came out every day to make fun of Israel and Israel's God, no one had the guts to fight—until David heard what was happening.

David didn't have to think twice. He couldn't stand hearing Goliath say all those horrible things against the God he loved and served. "God will protect me from Goliath and help me win, just as He has helped me many times against the wild animals that have attacked my sheep," David explained to King Saul and the others. They finally agreed, and the rest is history. With a single smooth stone shot from his sling, David struck Goliath in the head and finished him off with Goliath's own sword (1 Samuel 17).

Do you feel too small or young or untalented to do anything great in life? Then remember David, but not just for the Goliath

encounter. David's faith in God was so strong because he had learned how to trust God in the smaller daily tests of life. Today, look for God at work in your life, teaching you to lean on Him for strength. Age and size don't matter when you're standing on God's side.

PRAYER POINTER

Father, help me learn to love and trust You like David so that I'm ready to stand strong for You when the time comes.

The Woman of Wisdom

But if any of you needs wisdom,
you should ask God for it.

James 1:5

Solomon was the wisest man who ever lived. But the queen of Sheba showed her own intelligence when she left her kingdom in search of the source of Solomon's great wisdom. She wanted to know God so that she, too, could rule her kingdom better (2 Chronicles 9:1–8).

Solomon didn't disappoint her. And neither will God disappoint you when you seek to understand and know Him more. The queen of Sheba lets us know that treasures like wisdom and character are far more precious than gold or silver, and they are worth our effort and energy to seek them from their source: God.

So how do you seek wisdom from God? Just ask Him. God says He is glad to give us all that we need so that we can walk through this life with confidence in whom we are and what we are doing. God Himself is our treasure, the greatest reward for seeking to live a life that honors and pleases Him.

Prayer Pointer

Jesus, all wisdom comes from You. Please give me
understanding so that I will follow all of Your ways.

The King Who Repented

How can a young person live a pure life?
He can do it by obeying your word.

Psalm 119:9

King Josiah was crowned at age eight and worked hard to do what was right in God's sight. One day, while his workers were repairing God's temple, they discovered the book of the Law. The high priest sent it to Josiah, and Josiah realized just how far God's people had gone from His ways. Josiah tore his robe and cried before God in repentance. Huldah, a woman prophetess, told Josiah that his tender heart toward God had pleased Him. Though the kingdom of Judah would be destroyed for its sin, Josiah would live in peace and not have to witness it in his lifetime (2 Kings 22).

God takes sin very seriously because He is a perfect and holy God. Fortunately, we don't have to behave perfectly for God to love us. But we do need to walk in Josiah's footsteps. To know how to honor God, we must study His Word and apply it by obeying Him and repenting with a soft heart whenever we learn we've wandered from the truth.

Prayer Pointer

Father, please create in me a heart that
responds to what You say.

The One Who Pondered

Continue to think about the things that are good and worthy of praise. Think about the things that are true and honorable and right and pure and beautiful and respected.

Philippians 4:8

For just an ordinary Hebrew girl, Mary had already seen some pretty incredible things in her young teen life. Out of nowhere, an angel appeared to her, telling her she was going to have a baby by the power of God's Holy Spirit. God also sent an angel to explain things to Joseph, the man she was soon to marry. But the strangeness didn't stop there. God chose for Mary to have the baby Jesus in Bethlehem, a town far from their home, in a cold stable where an animal trough became the baby bed for God's Son. Suddenly, a bunch of smelly shepherds showed up, asking if they could worship Jesus! Mary's head must have been spinning with all the wild things happening to and around her. But she knew that God was in control, and the Bible says she pondered all these things in her heart (Luke 1:26–38; 2:1–19).

Do you know what it means to ponder? It means she was thinking about all that was going on and considering how God planned to use these events to help His people.

Do you have unusual circumstances in your life? Instead of just

going through your day without taking special notice, ponder those events in your heart like Mary did. What do you think God is showing you? Where is He leading you? How is God using that situation to bring you closer to Him in faith and trust?

Prayer Pointer

Father, nothing happens to me by accident because
You are in control of all things. Give me eyes to see
You and a heart that thinks about who You are.

Elizabeth

The Woman Who Listened

"THose wHo believe witHout seeing
me will be tRuly Happy."

JoHN 20:29

E ver since he came out of the tabernacle, Zechariah—Elizabeth's husband and a priest—had been acting strange. He could motion with his hands, but no words were coming out of his mouth. Turns out, an angel had told Zechariah that he was going to be a father, but Zechariah didn't believe him. God wasn't too happy about that, so Zechariah lost the ability to speak for a while.

Zechariah and Elizabeth's child was no ordinary child. The baby boy became John the Baptist, the man God chose to prepare the world for His coming Son, Jesus. Unlike Zechariah, Elizabeth immediately believed the good news and celebrated God's goodness to her. When Elizabeth's baby was born, they named him John in obedience to the angel's instructions, and Zechariah got his speech back (Luke 1).

Even though some of the rules or instructions in God's Word might seem too difficult to follow or too different from the norm, Elizabeth's story reminds us that living life God's way might not make sense at the time. But if we trust Him fully, God will lead us into the wonderful plans He has for our lives.

PRayeR PointeR

Lord, Your understanding is greater than mine.
Please help me trust You by following Your Word.

The One Who Worshipped

Praise Him, you servants of the Lord.

Psalm 135:1

Mary, Martha, and Lazarus—a family near and dear to Jesus—had already learned and seen so much from the Teacher. Earlier, Martha had learned that it was better to sit at Jesus' feet and listen than to tire herself out with unnecessary preparations. All of them had witnessed the miracle of Jesus raising Lazarus from the dead. And now they were all together again with Jesus, eating dinner.

But Mary took her love and devotion even deeper. Taking a jar of very expensive perfume, she broke it open and poured it on Jesus' feet, wiping it with her own hair. Her act showed how honored she felt to be in Jesus' presence and how much she loved and valued Him. Even though Jesus' apostle Judas thought it was a waste, Jesus said it was beautiful (John 12:1–8).

More than anything God wants our hearts. When we humble ourselves and worship Him, we touch God's heart—whether that's with perfume like Mary or with songs and dancing like King David or by falling down in prayer and praise like the angels around God's throne. Are you willing to show Him your love with your life and your praise?

Prayer Pointer

Father, You love it when we praise You. Fill
my heart and mouth with Your praise.

The One Who Wished Well

Jesus answered, "I am the way. And
I am the truth and the life. The only
way to the Father is through me."

JOHN 14:6

She had never seen Him before, the man beside Jacob's well. But when Jesus spoke to her, she couldn't resist His questions. "Will you give Me a drink?" He asked her.

She was startled because Jews, who hated Samaritans like her, never spoke with them. But before she knew it, Jesus was telling her about a kind of Living Water that He had but she didn't.

"Sir, where will You get that Living Water?" she wondered out loud. Then, when she learned it would quench her thirst forever, she begged, "Sir, give me this water!"

But Jesus wanted her to be honest first. He told her He knew that she had been with many men and that she wasn't married to the one she was with now. She had been looking for help and hope in people instead of God. But now Jesus was there, offering her life— Living Water—that would never go away.

She understood. She received the truth of Jesus. Then she ran to tell everyone back in town to come talk to Jesus and find the truth for themselves. The Samaritan woman who had been so thirsty for

hope had been filled to overflowing with the love of Jesus, and she had to share it with everyone (John 4:5–42).

Do you know the love of Jesus like the woman at the well? Are you amazed that God can and does forgive all your sins and promises you eternal life with Him in heaven? Then let that good news and great love flow out of you like Living Water, refreshing every person God puts in your path.

Prayer Pointer

Jesus, You fill my life with every good thing.
Help me share the goodness with others.

Tabitha

The One Who Served

I will show you my faith by the things I do.

James 2:18

Tabitha had been very busy. She worked with the widows of Joppa, making robes and clothes and helping the poor people around her with all the energy she had. But one day, Tabitha died unexpectedly. Her widow friends were so sad! They had washed her body and put it upstairs to await burial when they remembered that Peter was in town. They sent for him, and Peter came.

He asked everyone to leave. Then he knelt beside Tabitha and prayed. Peter said, "Tabitha, get up." And she did! Tabitha was raised back to life to continue her life of love and service to God and His people (Acts 9:36–42).

Now take a moment to think about your life. What do you spend most of your time doing? Are you using your energy to serve God and help others, or do you spend it just on yourself? Ask God to give you a heart like Tabitha's, and start looking for little ways that you can make the most of your day today.

Prayer Pointer

Lord, You have asked us to care for the poor, widowed, and orphaned. Show me how I can help.

Can you think of any other Bible characters who might be surprising beauties or beaus? What about their stories makes them unique?

_____

_____

_____

_____

_____

_____

_____

_____

_____

_____

_____

DIVINE DESIGN

Precious Pearls

We have small troubles for a while now, but they are helping us gain an eternal glory. That glory is much greater than the troubles.

2 Corinthians 4:17

Have you ever held a real pearl in your hand? Looking at such beauty, it's tough to even imagine how it was made.

God saw fit to have rough, gray oysters make valuable, lustrous pearls. Inside the oyster's hard, bumpy shell lies a soft and slippery body that looks and feels like a detached tongue (gross!). When an irritant like a grain of sand or microscopic bacteria gets inside the shell, the oyster responds by coating it with *nacre*, the same chemical it uses to make the "mother of pearl" lining inside its shell. As it keeps coating and recoating the intruder, a beautiful pearl is formed!

Did you know that God uses irritants in your life to grow beauty inside you too? Maybe you have a brother who bothers you. Or your family struggles with money. Maybe your parents got divorced. Everyone has problems. But each time we trust God to help us with our problems, we are like the oyster coating the sand. Before you know it, your life will be a beautiful, shining example of God's beauty for the whole world to see.

Prayer Pointer

Jesus, thank You for using even my problems
to make me beautiful in Your sight.

True Colors

"WHEN THE RAINBOW APPEARS IN THE CLOUDS,
I will see it. THEN I will REMEMBER THE
AGREEMENT THAT CONTINUES FOREVER."

GENESIS 9:16

Try this experiment on a sunny day: get a glass of water (or a crystal vase or pendant) and a plain white piece of paper, and go to the window. Try holding the glass or prism at different places just above the paper in front of the window. What do you see? If you find the right position, a rainbow will appear on your paper! Your glass is clear, and the sun is white, so where are all those colors coming from? Even though your eyes can't detect it, the white light shining through your window is actually made up of all those colors. When light passes through the glass, the water droplets bend it, separating the white light into a beautiful display of color.

Rainbows show the difference between how we see ourselves and how God sees us. We may think we are ordinary people with nothing special about us. But when God is in us, it's like the light shining through the glass. Suddenly we—and everyone around us—can see who we really are. Our lives are colored with His love, joy, and peace, and it is a beautiful sight for all to see.

PRAYER POINTER

Lord, please shine the light of Your love through
me and make me beautiful in Your sight!

The Light Switch

> Your word is like a lamp for my
> feet and a light for my way.
> Psalm 119:105

C an you imagine our world without light? Why don't you try an experiment with a friend? Let your friend go in another room and set up some objects that you haven't seen, like books, pictures, flowers, or a spice jar. Next, have your friend turn off all the lights and put a blindfold around your eyes. Carefully explore the room using your other senses, like touch and smell, to help you figure out what the objects are and identify them to your friend. When you are satisfied with your investigation, turn on the lights, and remove the blindfold. How did you do? Were you able to correctly identify each item, or did some of them confuse you?

God never meant for His people to stumble around in darkness. He gives us light to enjoy the beauty of what He has made. And spiritually, God's Word is a light that helps us see what's going on in people's hearts and lives. So don't stumble around in darkness, missing the beauty of who God is and who He has made you to be. Turn on the light of His Word!

Prayer Pointer

Father, thank You for the Bible. It helps me
know You and how I fit in Your plan.

Small Wonder

"WHEN you aRe weak, tHeN my
poweR is made peRfect iN you."

2 CoRiNtHiaNs 12:9

Out of the corner of your eye, you see a flash of green and black whizz by. At first glance, the hummingbird looks like a fragile, impossibly small bird with a long beak that stretches nearly the length of its entire body. But did you know that hummingbirds have an amazing memory? They can remember not only each flower they have visited but also how long it will take for that flower's nectar to refill. And when a hummingbird takes flight, its wings flap so fast you can't even see them move. Zipping and diving, hovering and even flying backward, it's easy to see that God packed a lot of power and skill into this tiny package.

God does the very same thing with you. It doesn't matter if you feel too young or small to make a difference in your world. God has packed you with amazing power and skill—coming from His own Spirit in you! Like a hummingbird looks for blooming flowers, you are to look for people who need God's love. God will give you everything you need to spread the joy of His love all around you, making the world a more beautiful place.

PRayeR PoiNteR

Thank You, Lord, that Your grace and power in me
make me strong and able to do Your work.

Let It Snow

> Take away my sin, and I will be clean. Wash
> me, and I will be whiter than snow.
>
> Psalm 51:7

The night before, the yard outside your kitchen window looked brown and drab with leafless, gray trees standing tall and empty against an overcast sky. But this morning, a miracle happened! Beautiful white snow blankets the ground, covering branches, glistening in the sun, and reflecting light back into beautiful blue skies. Here are some interesting facts about the snow you might not know:

- Snow isn't really white. It's clear! It's just the way light reflects off of it that makes it appear white.
- Each snowflake is made up of around two hundred ice crystals and has six sides.
- Snow falls around three to four miles per hour from the sky.
- Billions of snowflakes fall in an average snowstorm.

So why do you think God gave us snow? Yes, it's perfect for making snowmen and snow angels. But have you ever thought that God wanted you to see a picture of His love in the snow? God says that all of us have sin in our hearts—dark, ugly sin (kind of like those empty trees and brown grass in the winter yard). But when we admit our sin and tell God that we need His forgiveness, the Bible says He washes our hearts even whiter than snow! Our lives take on a whole new look, one that is clean and beautiful, reflecting God's light back into the world.

Jesus, thank You for forgiving me and
making my heart whiter than snow!

Craft: Let It Snow... All Year Long!

Since you can't really keep snow all year round, why not make this cool keepsake as a reminder?

What You Need:

- A clear plastic soda or water bottle
- A knife
- Glue
- Glitter
- String or yarn
- Q-tips or paint brush

Directions:

1. Have a parent cut the bottom off the bottle (about two inches from the bottom).
2. Cut a small hole in the top to hang a string.
3. Paint glue in desired places inside the bottle.
4. Sprinkle glitter in the glue.
5. If you want more colors, let the glue dry, and then repeat the process, painting other areas of the bottle.
6. Hang it up, and you have a beautiful, glittery reminder of God's amazing love and forgiveness.

And I know that you now have that
same faith. That is why I remind
you to use the gift God gave you.

2 Timothy 1:5-6

Did you know that vanilla extract comes from a bean that grows from an orchid vine? Originally discovered in Mexico, these delicate vines produce orchid flowers that bloom only for a single day. In order for pollination to occur so that beans can grow, something has to target that bloom at just the right time, lift up a special flap on the anther that houses the pollen, and press it to the stigma that pollinates the flower. But what on earth would know how to do all that at just the right time?

The Melipona bee does! These tiny bees, some no larger than a flea, are able to find the orchids, lift the flap, and transfer the pollen, all in the nick of time. Without these amazing creatures, the vanilla bean would have become extinct long ago.

Like the Melipona bee, God has created you for a very special purpose: to be His child! As you follow God, He will lead you to the special work He has planned for you, and He promises that every-where you go, you will spread the fragrance and flavor of God's great goodness.

Prayer Pointer

Father, everything You have made has a special
purpose, including me. Thank You!

Seek those things which are above.

Colossians 3:1 KJV

Who do you look up to?

If you lived in the savanna regions of Africa, you would often look up to giraffes, the tallest mammals in the world that live there. With six-foot legs, a six-foot neck, and feet the size of dinner plates, these lanky, spotted animals lumber around the savanna searching for food from up high, where the thickest and best acacia leaves grow. To fuel their large bodies, giraffes eat up to one hundred pounds of leaves each day! Since not many predators can tackle creatures their size, they can live up to twenty-five years, even in the wild.

But giraffes aren't the only ones who need to look up for food. We do too! God tells us that He is more nourishing to our souls than any food found on earth. If we want our spiritual bodies to grow tall and strong, we need to feed on heavenly things—the truths we find in God's Word. Just like giraffes eat lots of food every day, we also need to look for God in His Word every day. Standing tall and strong, we will be better able to fight off Satan and any other forces that try to come against us.

Prayer Pointer

Lord, help me keep my eyes focused
on You. Feed me Your truth.

Summer Storms

You are my hiding place. You protect me from
my troubles. You fill me with songs of salvation.

Psalm 32:7

*C*rash! You are jolted awake by a thundering sound. *Flash!* A
bright light illuminates the night sky outside your window.
And then you hear the sound of rain, slow at first, but even-
tually pouring all around outside. Grateful for the shelter of your
house, you snuggle deeper under the covers, waiting for the storm
to be over.

Storms can be very scary sometimes, can't they? Storms can
make us feel powerless and vulnerable, even though we know that
the rain is good for watering and growing the earth.

But storms can be good for something else too: reminding us
of God's tremendous power! As big as storms get and as strong as
the lightning seems, God is even bigger and stronger because He
not only made the world that houses those storms, He created the
universe, which holds everything else! Our God is really, really big
and powerful. And He says that He is the perfect place of shelter for
His people when storms come—not just rain storms, but storms of
life, like sickness, sadness, or separation. God welcomes us to come
to Him whenever we are afraid, and He will keep us safe in His care!

Prayer Pointer

Father, thank You for watching over
me and keeping me safe.

Crabby Habits

Wear God's armor so that you can fight against the devil's evil tricks.

Ephesians 6:11

Have you ever waded in the surf searching for seashells only to find one with a crab-like creature inside? If so, you have discovered a hermit crab, an amazing ten-legged creature that many people keep as pets. But did you know that hermit crabs don't grow their own shells? They actually borrow shells from sea snails, who make them. So when they outgrow their shells, hermit crabs molt, meaning they switch to larger shells. Then the soft hermit crab is vulnerable to predators.

Just like hermit crabs, we are soft and vulnerable to our enemy, Satan, who would love to destroy us. But God has provided us a "shell" too: the armor of God, which protects His people from worldly predators. You can read all about it in Ephesians 6, where God describes the belt of truth, breastplate of righteousness, sword of the Spirit, helmet of salvation, shield of faith, and shoes of the gospel of peace. As long as we cover ourselves with the truth of God's Word and fight the lies of the enemy with God's sword—the Bible—we are protected and free to grow and encourage others to put on their special armor too.

Prayer Pointer

Jesus, thank You for giving us the armor of
God to help protect us from harm.

Better Sweet

YouR pRomises aRe so sweet to me.
THey aRe like HoNey to my moutH!

Psalm 119:103

Chocolate. Just the word itself conjures sweet thoughts of delicious candy bars and cookies. All over the world, no matter what language or culture, almost everyone loves the curious, dark delight. But where does it come from?

Believe it or not, chocolate grows on trees. Okay, not in the form of candy bars, but in large, ridged pods that grow directly out of the trunk of the Theobroma cacao tree. People have learned to harvest these pods and remove the white, pulpy insides (used for drinks and other things). But the seeds inside the pulp—the little black beans that taste absolutely bitter and horrible right out of the pod—are the secret to chocolate's success. Workers take the beans and ferment them, a process that makes the flavor taste more like the chocolate you know. After drying the beans for about a week, they are sent to factories that grind them and combine them with a lot of sugar to create that wonderful chocolate taste you love!

Did you know that people can be like the chocolate bean? By themselves, they are not very pleasant to be around and may make you want to leave them alone. But instead, try praying for them. God is able to change any heart so that others can taste and see how good God is.

PRayeR PointeR

Father, help me pray for others and share with
them the sweetness of Your friendship.

66

Bake: Tasting Is Believing

Can't believe chocolate starts off bitter? Try the transformation yourself. Follow this recipe for homemade brownies, and see how the right mix of ingredients makes all the difference!

What You Need:

1 1/2 cups all-purpose flour	2 large eggs
1/2 teaspoon baking powder	1 teaspoon vanilla extract
1/2 teaspoon baking soda	1 cup milk
1 1/4 cups sugar	1 cup chocolate chips
3/4 cup butter	
1/2 cup unsweetened cocoa powder	
(Go ahead and take a taste!)	

Directions:

Preheat the oven to 350 degrees. In a bowl stir together the flour, baking powder, and baking soda. Set aside. With your mom's help, combine the sugar, butter, and cocoa powder in a large saucepan, and cook over medium heat until the mixture melts, stirring constantly.

Remove from heat, and lightly beat in eggs and vanilla with wooden spoon. Alternate adding in the flour mixture and milk, mixing after each addition. Add in chocolate chips (or any other nut or candy you like), and spread batter into a greased 9 x 13-inch baking dish. Bake in oven for approximately 20 minutes. When sides appear cracked and dry, remove from oven, and let cool. Cut and enjoy your chocolate creation!

> [God's] mercies never stop. They are new
> every morning. LORD, your loyalty is great.
>
> Lamentations 3:23-24

If you look all around the creation God has made, His incredible creativity is truly amazing. Flowers are just one of His defining details that paint our world with fragrance and beauty, showing us His character. One particularly interesting flower species is known as the morning glory. Unlike most flowers, morning glories unfurl when the morning sun warms their petals. As long as the sun shines down on them, the flowers remain open, revealing a wide variety of colors. But as evening approaches and the sun fades, the petals slowly curl and close up until the next day.

Did you know our spiritual hearts are a little like the morning glory? On our own in a cold, dark world, we stay closed up and afraid to be ourselves or to reach out to other people. But when we realize that God's love is shining down on us, we open up to Him, showing Him and the world the beautiful person He has made us to be. We grow and flourish as long as we stay in God's light. And every day is a new day to soak up the warmth of His love.

Prayer Pointer

Lord, Your love comforts me and helps me open
up to be the person You made me to be.

Slug Sleuth

> People look at the outside of a person,
> but the LORD looks at the heart.
>
> 1 Samuel 16:7

It's time to test your slug knowledge. (Betcha didn't think anybody would say that to you today.) Look at the facts below, and circle the ones you think are true.

A. Slugs have more teeth than sharks.

B. Slug blood is green.

C. Slugs can slide over razor blades or cut glass without getting hurt because of their slime.

D. To find their way home, slugs leave a scent trail.

E. Slugs will eat just about anything.

If you circled all the answers, you are correct! Who would have thought something so gross-looking could have so many skills?

The slug actually shows us some important truths. You can't judge animals—or people—based on what they look like on the outside. Every person God makes has a special part to play in this great big world He is running, so ask God to help you appreciate and respect everyone He has made.

Prayer Pointer

God, Your creativity and love are endless.
When I'm respecting and loving others, I
am respecting and loving You too.

"If a person believes in me, rivers of living water will flow out from his heart."

JOHN 7:38

Can you imagine what our world would be like without water? No oceans, rivers, or lakes. No clouds in the sky or rain. And even no swimming pools! But water doesn't just gather in large places; water also fills all living things. In fact, 50 to 65 percent of each person on earth is made of water. Plants and animals are made up of a large percentage of water as well. So take away water, and you take away the world and every living thing in it.

So, yeah, you could say water is *really* important. It's also cool how God not only created water but keeps it fresh and useful as it cycles from rain to streams to nourishing the earth, evaporating and condensing in clouds to start the cycle again.

Remember when Jesus was talking with a Samaritan woman at Jacob's well? She was interested in drawing well water, but Jesus told her He had something better: Living Water! He went on to explain that Jesus Himself is that Living Water. More than people need water to live, we need Jesus to fill our lives with His presence so that we can grow and live and love the way we were meant to.

Prayer Pointer

Jesus, I need You more than water. Please fill me with Your Spirit so I can truly live.

"I am the vine, and you are the branches.
If a person remains in me and I remain
in Him, then He produces much fruit.
But without me He can do nothing."

JOHN 15:5

What do wind, water, and the sun have in common? They can all be used to produce electricity! You know, that curious element you use when you watch TV, turn on lights, or curl your hair.

Even though we might not totally understand what it is, how it gets to our homes, or how it powers our appliances, we are certainly glad it does. But what happens when there is a break in the connection, like when a plug gets pulled out of the wall or lightning knocks out the power lines? It stops working, and we can't get our normal work done.

God wants us to know that He is our biggest power source. As long as we stay plugged into Him by reading His Word, obeying Him, and talking to Him through prayer, we will be filled with His energy and power to do the work He has created us to do. If you feel powerless today, plug into God through prayer. He will give you the strength and wisdom you need for each day.

Prayer Pointer

Father, I know that I can't do anything apart
from You. Help me stay connected to You.

Seeing Is Deceiving

> "People look at you and think you are good. But
> on the inside you are full of hypocrisy and evil."
>
> Matthew 23:28

Nestled in a balmy rainforest of Indonesia is a species of the world's biggest flowers: the Rafflesia. In full bloom, the Rafflesia's large red petals stretch three feet across. Little white specks mark the five petals that surround a large, circular center. But step closer, and you'll notice something else: the Rafflesia has a *horrible* smell. This beautiful, enormous flower smells like rotting flesh, which is why it's also called the "corpse flower." This foul odor attracts carrion flies, which help pollinate other Rafflesias.

Don't want a Rafflesia in your garden anymore? Well, we don't want to be like one either. In the Bible, Jesus warns that people who follow rules just so they can look good and be praised by others are like empty tombs. Like the Rafflesia, they look good on the outside, but they are full of rottenness inside (Matthew 23:27).

How do you get the rotten stuff out so that you can be a fragrant flower for God? Ask Him to change you and help you be honest about how much you need Him. Then choose to follow God because it pleases Him, no matter what anyone else says or thinks. He will make you bloom into a fragrant child of God.

Prayer Pointer

Lord, keep me from only pretending to love You.
Make my life real and beautiful in Your eyes.

Break the Mold

"So if the Son makes you free,
then you will be truly free."

JOHN 8:36

Imagine for a moment a creature about the size of a cat. Now picture that animal covered in otter fur with four webbed feet, similar to a duck. Put a duck bill on its face, just below its small ears and eyes. Now add a beaver tail and some sharp spurs on the hind feet capable of injecting toxic venom. Sound like something out of an odd fairy tale? Actually, you've just imagined what a platypus, a real mammal found in Australia and Tasmania, looks like! Unlike most mammals, platypuses are monotremes—they lay eggs instead of birthing their babies live.

Platypuses are fun reminders to the rest of us that being different—even quirky—can be really cool. Often, people like to dress the same, talk the same, and do the same kind of activities as everyone else so they fit in. But isn't that kind of boring? Like the platypus, we can enjoy being exactly who God made us to be, even if it doesn't fit the mold of what everyone else is like. We are free to be ourselves, keeping our eyes on the One who created us and living for His glory and approval alone.

Prayer Pointer

God, thank You for making Your world so creatively. I want
to be everything You meant for me to be—for Your glory!

Inner Power

"I will put my spirit inside you. And
I will help you live by my rules. You
will be careful to obey my laws."

Ezekiel 36:27

How would you like a bed made out of saliva? No thanks? Well, you must not be a baby electric eel then. The bed of saliva formed by the male electric eel makes the perfect place for the female to lay over seventeen thousand eggs. Electric eels have an electricity-producing organ inside them that takes up around eighty percent of their body, making them able to produce up to six hundred volts of electricity whenever they are being attacked or when they are hunting prey. That's enough electricity to light twelve light bulbs five times stronger than the electric sockets in your home!

While electric eels look like most ordinary eels, they have a secret source of power inside that the others don't. Christians, too, look like ordinary people. We wear clothes and talk and walk, just like people who don't know God. But the difference lies within us. When we place our faith in Jesus, God puts His Spirit inside of us, filling us with His amazing power. Why not shock the people around you with the remarkable power of God's love for them today?

Prayer Pointer

Father, because of Your power in me, I am
empowered to live well for You. Thank You!

"You hear the wind blow. But you don't
know where the wind comes from or where
it is going. It is the same with every
person who is born from the Spirit."

JOHN 3:8

You feel it all around you as summer closes and autumn's
arrival turns the trees into a vibrant palette of color. Cool
wind brushes your skin and bends the trees that sway with
its presence.

Really, wind is no mystery. As the sun heats the earth's atmo-
sphere, warm air rises. At the same time, cold air is falling downward.
As that new air is heated, the process continues, leaving our planet
with the wonderful phenomenon of wind.

Isn't it interesting that everybody believes wind exists, even
though they don't understand everything about it and they can't see
it with their eyes? If only everyone would view God from the same
perspective. Like the wind, God can't be seen with our eyes. But we
can certainly see what He does—just look around at the incredible
creation. Only a great Designer could do that. And how about love?
Prized in every culture around the world, love's virtues point to a
Creator who designed us all to love Him and one another. Whenever
you feel the wind, whisper a word of thanks to the unseen God who
made it and you too!

=== Prayer Pointer ===

Father, even though I can't see You, I feel You working in
me, and I see what wonderful works You have done.

Crawling to Glory

God began doing a good work in you.
And He will continue it until it is finished
when Jesus Christ comes again.

Philippians 1:6

Migrating monarchs make an extraordinary sight. Tens of thousands of these brilliant black and orange insects take to the sky from southern California and Mexico and head north. Once they reach their destination and deposit their eggs on milkweed leaves, the butterflies die. But soon, the eggs hatch, and caterpillars emerge. Once caterpillars mature, they form chrysalises—cocoons to house their bodies as they undergo an amazing transformation. At the right time, the once-caterpillars break out of the chrysalises as wonderfully winged butterflies! The monarchs then seek out mates, lay eggs, and the cycle repeats itself. But during the fourth generation, the monarchs don't die! Instead, they migrate back to California and Mexico, where their great-great-great-grandparents started. Isn't that a monumental monarch miracle?

As amazing as the monarch life cycle is, your life is a million times more miraculous. You are created in God's own image! Though you may or may not like what you see in the mirror, God is at work in you, changing you from the inside out. Just like the butterfly crawling from its chrysalis, you become a new creation when you give your life to Jesus. You were made to fly through this life with the warmth of God's love lifting your wings.

Prayer Pointer

Jesus, thank You for butterflies, and thank
You for making me a new creation too!

Lights, Camera, Action!

"The eye is a light for the body.
If your eyes are good, then your
whole body will be full of light."
Matthew 6:22

Did you know that you own one of the most complex cameras in the world? And it's sitting right on your face! Incredibly, your eye is designed so that light reflecting off objects you are looking at shines into your eye, past the sclera (the white outer part), through the cornea (clear), and to the pupil, which regulates the amount of light allowed in. Then the light passes through a lens, which curves or contracts to bend the light so the image is flipped and strikes the retina, where rods and cones absorb the light and send the message to your brain. Your brain reads the message, interpreting the image right side up, and lets your eyes know what you're seeing.

Sounds pretty complicated, doesn't it? It's just one of God's amazing creations that we don't necessarily understand but thoroughly enjoy. God has a lot to say about our eyesight. He wants us to remember that everything comes from Him, and when we keep our eyes focused on Him, we will have the wisdom to interact with this world in a way that pleases Him. Take time to thank Him for your eyes, and ask Him to help you maintain a clear focus on Him.

Prayer Pointer

Father, help me keep my focus on You as I enjoy
this incredible world You have made.

God used His infinite wisdom to design the
entire universe—including you! Can you
think of any special traits God gave you
to use while showing His love to others?

_____

_____

_____

_____

_____

_____

_____

_____

_____

_____

BODY BUILDERS

Mirror Makeover

You will be like a beautiful
crown in the LORD'S Hands.

Isaiah 62:3

What You Need:

- Dry erase markers • Clear tape • Piece of paper

Directions:

In your bathroom mirror, cover your face on the mirror with a piece of paper, and tape it in place. Now trace the outline of the paper with your dry erase marker. Remove the paper. (You should have a rectangle drawn on the mirror that frames your reflection.) Now decorate the outside of the border, helping your rectangle look like a picture frame. Using dry erase markers, write one of these verses below the frame so you will see it every day:

- I praise you because you made me in an amazing and wonderful way. What you have done is wonderful. I know this very well. Psalm 139:14
- God does not see the same way people see. People look at the outside of a person, but the Lord looks at the heart. 1 Samuel 16:7

Prayer Pointer

Dear God, thank You for making me in Your image as Your beautifully unique child. Help me to remember this truth every single day.

So comfort each other and
give each other strength, just
as you are doing now.

1 Thessalonians 5:11

uilding up others is an important part of being a Christian.
Read the following ten ways to comfort and help others.

1. Pray for God to help them know Him.
2. Give them a great big hug and a smile.
3. Write little notes that tell them you care, and stick them in special places where they'll find them.
4. Call them to see how they are doing.
5. Text them a Bible verse that has encouraged you.
6. Invite them to join you at church.
7. Cry with them when they are sad.
8. Celebrate their birthdays, victories, and accomplishments with balloons or banners or a special food treat.
9. Ask them how you can help them or pray for them.
10. Remind them every day how much you and God love them!

Prayer Pointer

God, help me to actively seek You, and
help me help those around me.

> Early the next morning, Jesus woke and left the house while it was still dark. He went to a place to be alone and pray.
>
> Mark 1:35

f God already knows what's going to happen, why pray? Circle your best guess.

A. God tells us to do it.

B. God's peace fills us when we do it.

C. Being still helps us remember who God is.

D. God says that He is with us when we pray together.

E. God listens when we pray.

F. We grow closer and stay connected to God when we pray.

G. Prayer changes things. God says the prayers of His people are effective.

Well, did you circle them all? You should! Prayer is an extremely powerful weapon God has given us to fight off the enemy, to starve our fears, and to feed on God's incredible goodness. If you have God as your very best friend, why hold back? Learn these simple techniques to help you feel comfortable talking to your Creator all day, every day and experience the power His awesome presence brings to your day.

- Position: Find a quiet place where you can kneel or lie facedown before your King in prayer. The Bible also talks about lifting up your hands to heaven, even as a little girl lifts up her hands to be held by her daddy. This is your chance to reach out and receive by faith your Father's big hug.

- Prayer Cards: Sometimes our minds wander off track when we pray. To keep focused, prayer cards really help. Make a card for each person you want to pray for. Then list a Bible verse for each person and list any personal prayer requests you know that person has. Each day, choose one or two cards and talk to God about the needs you've listed there.
- Prayer Buddy: Find a friend who is comfortable talking to God too. Pick a time to get together and pray. After a while, you can learn how to pray with each other while you go for a walk or play.

--- Prayer Pointer ---

God, I am so thankful You are always listening to my prayers. Please help me to always remember to turn to You with my needs and desires.

Be a woRkeR who is Not ashamed of
His woRk—a woRkeR who uses the
tRue teachiNg iN the Right way.

2 Timothy 2:15

If a snake crawled up to you and tried to convince you to disobey God, would you listen? After freaking out, saying "No!" would be the super easy part. Although Satan doesn't sneak up on people in serpent form anymore, he has some very successful ways to trip up God's people and keep others from life-saving truth. To make matters worse, our own sinful hearts often enjoy the lure of Satan's lies over the beauty of God's ways. So how can we stay on track with what's true?

God's Word! The Bible is God's letter to us that still packs amazing power for today's world. That's because the words in it all point to Jesus, building us up in our relationship with Him and His Spirit, who lives inside His people. But what good is a bunch of armor in battle if you never put it on and don't learn how to use it? Don't be a sitting duck. Gear up for the war games evil wages with our minds by learning God's truth first. Here's the plan of attack:

- Choose to memorize an entire passage of Scripture or book of the Bible one verse at a time.
- Locate a memory verse system. The Navigators have a good option on their website. If you have a smart phone or tablet, you can download apps like Fighter Verses that give you new verses to memorize each week, plus quizzes, songs, and clues to help the process.

- Create your own. Use Biblegateway.com or other online Bible search engines to look up verses that help you face the specific areas where you need help. Print out those verses or record them by hand on notecards that can be kept in a recipe box, separated into the seven days of the week. Each day, study the verse listed on that card until you have it memorized. Then move it to the back of the box, where you can review those verses once a week or month. Then add a new verse and card to fill in that day.

Then find a parent or friend who will test you on your verses and recite them out loud. It will help them stick in your memory.

Over time, your mind will be strengthened by knowing God and His truth. When the enemy comes to try to trick you into following him, God's Spirit will help you remember what you've learned and help you answer evil just like Jesus did—with God's own words of truth.

PRayeR PoiNteR

God, help me to commit Your Word to memory,
and help me to always turn to it for guidance.

If you have any message that will encourage the people, please speak!

Acts 13:15

Becoming an encourager isn't always easy. But the more you do it, the more natural it will feel, and the better encourager you will become. Look up the Scripture passage listed, and write out at least one way you could encourage those around you!

- (Isaiah 1:17) At school, you notice some bullies picking on the new kid. You could pretend you didn't see it and go play somewhere else, but instead you

_____

- (1 Peter 4:10) Your mom is tired but still has to make dinner. You're tired too and could go to your room. Or you could

_____

- (1 Thessalonians 1:2) Every day your parents go to work so they can make the money your family needs to live. Today you decide to show them how much you appreciate what they do, so you

_____

Prayer Pointer

Father, help me see people the way You do, and
help me remember to treat them with love.

WHICH of these was your favorite
activity? WHY did the lesson
you learned stick with you?

_____

_____

_____

_____

_____

_____

_____

_____

_____

CHARACTER QUEST

Love in Action

"One must love His neighbor as He loves Himself."

Mark 12:33

You've probably heard Jesus' famous command, "Love your neighbor as yourself." But what does that really look like? Jesus explained that "neighbor" means anyone God brings into your life. But to put the idea into practice, pick one of your actual neighbors this week, and choose from the following:

- Make a meal that you like to help your mom prepare, or bake cookies, then take the food over.
- Write a card that tells your neighbors how much you and God love them.
- With your mom's permission and help, offer to babysit so they can have a night out.
- Plant an herb or vegetable garden in your backyard. Make regular visits to talk with your neighbors, and give them fresh herbs and vegetables.

Keep a journal of your visits. Each time, answer the following questions:

- How did it make you feel to love your neighbors this way?
- How did they respond?
- How can you pray for them?
- What other ideas to love others well come to your mind?

Prayer Pointer

God, help me to remember to bless
my neighbors with Your love.

Growing Gratitude

Give thanks whatever happens.

1 Thessalonians 5:18

We know we're supposed to give thanks at meals and probably before we go to sleep. But did you know that God wants us to give thanks in all things? That's right! Giving thanks to God for whatever happens in our lives shows that we trust Him and that we know every good gift comes from Him. God even uses the tough times in our lives for our good so we can thank Him for those too.

Growing a thankful heart is a lot like growing a tree. Ask God to plant seeds of thankfulness in your heart. But don't just let them sit there. Water and nourish them by noticing the little acts of kindness all around you. Look at the incredible creation God has made, and marvel at the clouds, the creatures, and all the creativity they show of God and thank Him.

Write down specific things for which you are really thankful. Keep each description to a few words, like "my dog," "my heartbeat," or "God's Word." How many can you find today? Tomorrow? The next day?

Be on the alert, ready to write something down as soon as you spot evidence of God's smile in your day. Then read your list back to God, and thank Him for His everlasting goodness.

Prayer Pointer

Jesus, please keep me from complaining.
Help me give thanks in all things.

Secret Service

"In the same way, the Son of Man did not come to be served. He came to serve. The Son of Man came to give His life to save many people."

Mark 10:45

Jesus didn't have to come. He could have stayed in the comfort of heaven where He ruled as King, served by obedient and honoring angels for the rest of all time. But He didn't. His love for us drove Him to come to earth to live, serve, and even die so that we could be with Him forever. Can you imagine that kind of cost? Yet giving our lives for others—serving their needs instead of our own—is exactly what God's kind of love makes us want to do.

Do you have Jesus' Spirit living in you? Then you get the joy of experiencing the secret-service life that Jesus did. Everywhere you look, there are opportunities to encourage others, pray, comfort, give, and help meet needs. But the mission starts with prayer, asking God to open your eyes to see it and help you act just like Jesus. So why not ask Him for that right now? If you do, then you're ready for your first mission. Remember, though, this is secret service. Don't tell them what you're planning to do or why (just yet). Only God and you will know the plan.

Pick a family member you want to target this week. Spend the first day just watching what he or she does, looking for ways you could serve and love that person better. Ask God for creativity, and mark an X by the ideas that you want to try this week:

- [ ] Each day this week, tell them something encouraging about themselves.
- [ ] Help with the laundry, or put away laundry for someone.
- [ ] Clean out the car, or take out the trash each day.
- [ ] Volunteer to read a book or play a game with a younger sibling.
- [ ] Your own idea: _____

_____

Record to Remember

1. Was the mission a success?
2. How did it make you feel?
3. How did your target person react? Do you wish they would have responded differently (been more thankful or noticed more)?
4. How does this exercise help you know how to respond when others serve you?

Next week's mission: Pick a new family member or friend, and repeat the process. And keep on serving the one from last week too!

Prayer Pointer

Father, I'm so glad You give me opportunities to serve those around me. Help me to serve with a cheerful, thankful heart.

Your beauty should come from within
you—the beauty of a gentle and quiet
spirit. This beauty will never disappear,
and it is worth very much to God.

1 Peter 3:4

Some people just seem to come by having a quiet spirit naturally. Nothing appears to make them angry or upset. But others of us aren't wired that way. When things don't go according to our plan, we can explode in frustration or anger. Or when our parents, teachers, or really anybody tells us what to do, we feel like it's time to take up our battle weapons and fight them with all we've got.

It seems unfair. How can Jesus want *all* of us to have a gentle and quiet spirit? Because Jesus isn't asking us to change our personalities. He just wants us to let His Spirit rule over them! A gentle and quiet spirit is someone—with any personality—who has learned to obey God by loving Him and others, no matter how loud and talkative or quiet and reserved he or she is on the outside. God has the power to help all of us respond to life's challenges in a way that honors Him, a beautiful reflection of His wonderful Spirit working in us. We just need to pray and ask Him to help us see where our spirits are getting too loud (telling God what we're going to do) and make them quiet (choosing to obey God's Spirit instead).

So what does a gentle and quiet spirit look like? Circle the answers that show God's beauty best.

- Your sister runs ahead of you to get in the front seat. You:

    A. Run to catch up and try to push your way into the seat.
    B. Graciously take the backseat without complaining.

- Your parents have other plans, and they are not allowing you to spend the night with your friend. You:

    A. Angrily go to your room, where you think about how mean your parents are.
    B. Trust God with the change of plans and find something else to do.

- You really love the beat and tune to this song, but you know the lyrics are really bad. You

    A. Listen to it anyway because you figure you can just ignore the words.
    B. Find another song that doesn't dishonor God.

Can you think of any times when you want to do one thing, but God wants something else? Write them here: _____

_____

_____

Prayer Pointer

Lord, please create in me a gentle and quiet
spirit that is of great worth in Your sight.

> "Those who work to bring peace are happy."
>
> Matthew 5:9

So, you know it's a good thing to be a peacemaker. You've probably been told this more than a thousand times at home and school. But have you ever wondered why God wants His people to be keepers of His peace?

Maybe it's easier to think about the opposite of peace: war. Fighting shows a break in togetherness. People are always divided in fights. But God did not create people to be against each other or Him. His plan is for His people to be one big, happy family, serving Him and loving each other. What keeps that from happening now? Sin! Ever since sin entered our world with Adam and Eve, people have been separated from each other and God. It was an important enough problem to God that He sent Jesus to die (and rise again) so that we could be at peace with Him and others again. One day, when we're all in heaven, we will see God's big plan in full action. We will all love Him and each other in perfect unity.

But for now, God wants each of us to play our role in keeping peace here on earth. It helps other people see God's plan and want to be with Him too, so it's a really important job for us. But how do we do it? Pray, and ask God for wisdom. Then think about some of the situations below, and write a solution that stops the separation and starts the peace process.

Your friends at school have stopped speaking to each other because they are mad. You: _____

_____

Your family is arguing because they can't agree on a restaurant.
You: _____

_____

_____

Your sister, who is sitting beside you in church, keeps wanting to whisper and giggle during the sermon. You: _____

_____

_____

You got angry with your brother and said some pretty mean things during the fight. You: _____

_____

_____

You brought home the candy prize you won at school, but now your siblings want some. You: _____

_____

Your idea: _____

_____

─────────── PRayeR PoiNteR ───────────

Jesus, please give me Your peace. Help me
keep it daily in my life with others.

Taking Courage

Remember that I commanded you to be strong
and brave. So don't be afraid. The LORD your
God will be with you everywhere you go.

JOSHUA 1:9

J oshua was facing some seriously scary stuff. Moses, Israel's trusted leader, had died. Now Joshua was supposed to lead that large group of people into the promised land, where many more people lived—people who hated the Israelites and wanted them destroyed.

God reminded Joshua: it doesn't matter what you face, God will give you the power to overcome when you follow Him. In other words, when we are on God's side, we can't fail. God wants us to live courageous and confident lives because we know He is our faithful Leader who never fails.

What would it look like for you to be strong and courageous? Maybe you will trust God to help you tackle the new trick in gymnastics that you have feared. Perhaps it's time you told your friends at school about your relationship with Jesus. Maybe it's something else.

One way you can grow bold and courageous like Joshua is to read about other believers who have lived a life that was confident in Christ. Learn from their examples, and ask the Lord to strengthen you in the same way. On the next page is a list of men and women who demonstrated amazing strength and courage in their commitment to Jesus. Pick one for this month, and ask your parents to help you locate a library book or find information online about this person. Then answer the questions that follow.

- Corrie Ten Boom
- Jim and Elisabeth Elliot
- Eric Liddell
- Amy Carmichael
- Billy Graham
- George Mueller
- Florence Nightingale
- C. S. Lewis
- Martin Luther
- Martin Luther King Jr.
- Bruce Olsen

What did this person do that was strong and courageous?

_____

_____

_____

How did God help him or her?

_____

_____

_____

How can this person's story help you to be strong and coura-geous too?

_____

_____

_____

=========== Prayer Pointer ===========

Jesus, I can be strong and courageous
because I know You're always with me.

Life or Death

"The words I told you are spirit,
and so they give life."

JOHN 6:63

Have you ever noticed how a single mean comment from a friend can ruin your whole day? On the other hand, a simple hug or encouraging word can make your spirit sing. Don't worry. We are all that way! God created us to respond to the power of words. It's one of the reasons God wrote the Bible for us. Through His words, we learn how to live life and find Jesus. God's words are powerful enough to change lives.

But your words are powerful too. Each time you open your mouth, you can choose to speak words that will help others know how valuable they are or how worthless you think they are. You can speak life to them or words of death. As very loved children of God, we no longer have any need to hurt others with our words. Instead, God has given us the mission to build others up, encouraging them in their faith and lives. But sometimes it can be very difficult, especially when that person or family member says mean things to you. It's natural to want to fight back. But it isn't God's way. God is love, and that's what He wants His kids to communicate to others at all times.

Look at the list of comments scattered on the next page. Which ones build up, and which ones tear down? Circle all the encouraging comments, and X out the ones that hurt.

You're doing great.

You're a lost cause.

That's okay; I mess up too.

You're not going to make it.

You're weird.

I forgive you.

Of course you failed.

I'm happy to help you.

You make me smile.

I can do better than you.

I hate you.

You look great.

I see Jesus in you.

You're an idiot.

You are such a great friend.

You're awesome.

I told you that you couldn't do it.

I appreciate you.

I love being with you.

How could you be so dumb?

I'm here for you.

Stay away from me.

Prayer Pointer

Jesus, fill my mouth with loving words that
come from Your heart and help others.

Humble Hearts

> Don't be too proud before the Lord,
> and He will make you great.
>
> James 4:10

You've seen it before. Maybe it was a rich kid in class who made another child feel bad for wearing unfashionable clothes. Or at church, perhaps there were people who acted like they were better than everybody else. Even at home, pride rears its ugly head when siblings or parents fight and then refuse to apologize or give in. Pride is the feeling that you are somehow better than another person and so deserve special treatment. In case you were wondering, God says He hates it (Amos 6:8).

What God loves, though, are people who are humble. Humility (being humble) is the exact opposite of being prideful. Humble people recognize how powerful and good God is and how much of a sinner they are. Strangely, understanding how bad we are helps us not only appreciate God's amazing grace more, but it also helps us see others with more compassion. Instead of looking at someone else and thinking how much better we are than them (for whatever reason), we simply see that everyone needs to know the love and forgiveness of Jesus as much as we do.

Speaking of Jesus, He is the One who gives us the best picture of humility. Read the passage from Philippians 2:6–9 on the next page. Then record all the ways you see Jesus thinking of others instead of Himself.

Christ himself was like God in everything. He was equal with God. But he did not think that being equal with God was something to be held on to.

He gave up his place with God and made himself nothing. He was born to be a man and became like a servant.

And when he was living as a man, he humbled himself and was fully obedient to God. He obeyed even when that caused his death—death on a cross.

So God raised Christ to the highest place. God made the name of Christ greater than every other name.

What did Jesus do to show humility?

_____

_____

What did God the Father do in response to Jesus?

_____

_____

Prayer Pointer

Father, please forgive my pride. I desperately
need You. You alone deserve glory.

Joy Full

THE LORD is my strength and shield. I
trust Him, and He helps me. I am very
happy. And I praise Him with my song.

Psalm 28:7

Look at the scenarios below. Circle the number beside the situations that you think could bring you joy.

1. A new puppy
2. Parents telling you what to do
3. An A on the test
4. Winning the game
5. Losing the game

6. Someone making fun of you
7. Chores at home
8. School work
9. Getting to go out to eat
10. Friends

So how many did you circle? If you didn't circle them all, you are missing out! The apostle Paul tells us that Christians look at life very differently from those who don't know God. Those who don't know God can only feel good about life when everything is going right. But God promises that every single thing that happens to one of His children was planned by Him to do us good (1 Thessalonians 5:16–18). Of course, tough times never *feel* good. But when we really believe that our loving Father has allowed the situation for our good—even though we don't understand how—then we find joy. Joy is a deep feeling of thankfulness, peace, and trust that comes from God's Spirit and grows every time we thank God for the good and bad times in life.

PRAYER POINTER

Jesus, teach me to trust You more so
that I can be full of Your joy.

Truth Telling

Jesus answered, "I am the way. And
I am the truth and the life."

JOHN 14:6

We know that we should tell the truth and lying is bad. But have you ever wondered why? Jesus says that when we tell a lie, we aren't talking like the children of God we are. Instead, we are acting like we belong to God's enemy, which is exactly what Satan wants. But when we speak the truth, we are talking God's language—and His words are powerful!

Look at the tempting situations below. Write out how you would respond with the truth.

- You accidentally broke your mom's necklace. You could hide it back in her jewelry drawer, but instead you:_____
_____.

- The kids at church were complaining that church was dumb. You want them to like you, but you don't agree with them. So you say: _____
_____.

- Your friend hurt your feelings when she ignored you at lunch. You could pretend everything was okay, but instead you bravely and lovingly tell her: _____.

It isn't always easy to tell the truth, but God will always strengthen you and help you do what's right when you ask Him.

Prayer Pointer

Lord, please keep me from telling lies, even in what
seem to be small ways. Make me truthful always.

Show mercy to others; be kind, humble, gentle, and patient.

Colossians 3:12

Microwaves help us cook entire meals in minutes. Computers put information from all over the world right at our fingertips the second we need to know it. Fast-food chains, cell phones, cars—you name it—all promise to make whatever we want to happen, happen faster.

So what happens when what we want doesn't happen right away? We get mad, of course! We huff and stomp our feet and try to force our way—no matter how it affects others. In other words, we are being impatient, the opposite of being patient. What is being patient? It is learning to let God control the schedule, allowing Him time to work in our lives.

Read the following stories, looking for examples of patience and impatience. Draw a *P* next to the example of patience and an *I* next to the example of impatience.

"Mom, I need to go to the store right now," Madeline said. "Honey, I'm right in the middle of making dinner," her mother replied. "But I have to get those jeans I told you about before school tomorrow," Madeline argued. "Have you saved enough money to buy them?" her mom asked. "No! But can we just go now anyway, and I'll pay you back later?" Madeline pressed. "Not right now, Honey," came the

final reply. "Humph!" Madeline grunted angrily and stomped off, slamming the door to her room.

The whole family had been in the car for what seemed an eternity. "Are we almost there yet?" Katelyn asked. "Got another hour to go," Dad answered. Katelyn was feeling very fidgety. A minute later she said, "What about now? How much time till we get there?" "About the same," came the reply. A few minutes passed, and Katelyn started to ask the question again, but something inside her told her not to speak. She prayed instead, asking God to help her pass the time. Suddenly, she remembered a fun car game she liked and asked her sister if she wanted to play. Engrossed in the game, the time flew by, and the family reached their destination.

PRAyeR PoiNteR

God, sometimes it's *so* difficult to wait for things I want. Please help me to remember all of the other blessings You've placed in my life while I wait patiently.

Getting to Give

"Give, aNd you will Receive. . . . THe way you
give to otHeRs is tHe way God will give to you."

Luke 6:38

I f you get your life information from TV shows or magazines, it
sure seems like getting more things is a lot better than giving up
things. After all, who wouldn't want more candy, more toys, more
clothes, more . . . whatever, right?

But Jesus warns us that what we think we want can actually
make us sick. The more we try to get things for ourselves, the more
miserable we become! For example, have you ever noticed how keeping a box of cookies to yourself instead of sharing them ruins your
appetite for healthy food, makes you feel gross, and leaves you feeling more alone? Why? Because God designed us to find our greatest
happiness in our friendship with Him, not by getting more things
for ourselves. The more we know and love God, the less we feel like
we need because we trust God, our Father, to take care of us. His
love frees us from the need to serve ourselves and makes us want to
give what we have to others because pleasing God is more fun than
getting stuff that only rots or breaks. Jesus says we get happiness
when we give.

Look at the scenarios that follow, and write in the blank how
you would turn these opportunities to get into ways to give:

Mom gave you an allowance for the week. You now have just
enough money to buy that bike you want, but you also know you
haven't given any of it at church. You decide to: _____
_____.

Your sister flew to you like a moth to a candle when she saw you brought home that bag of your favorite candy. There aren't a lot of pieces, so you decide to: _____

_____.

You had planned to spend the next hour watching your favorite show on TV when your brother asked if he could watch something else first. You know you could record your show, but you really wanted this time for yourself. You: _____

_____.

You are a really good artist, and everybody loves your work. You could just keep your talent to yourself, or you could: _____

_____.

Did you notice? Not only does God give us the chance to be generous (love giving) with our things but also with our time and talents! Everything we have belongs to God, and He loves for His kids to be cheerful givers, just like He is.

Prayer Pointer

Father, give me a generous heart that
loves to give like You do.

> "I love you people with a love that will last forever. I became your friend because of my love and kindness."
>
> Jeremiah 31:3

Take a minute, and think about your mom. Think about what her mornings before school are probably like. Can you guess? Imagine what she might be doing and thinking as she works while you are away. What must it be like to take care of kids and do laundry and work and cook and clean? What makes her happy or sad?

Congratulations! In the past minute, you have just exercised your unique ability to think about life from someone else's perspective. Instead of just thinking about what you do and what you think, you have started to think about the thoughts and needs of someone other than yourself. This important skill is called empathy. Empathy helps us learn how to love others better. Understanding others and thinking about their needs instead of just our own make us able to be kind. Being kind is caring for others according to their needs. The Bible says that when God's Spirit is ruling our hearts, we will be kind to others. Here are some examples of everyday situations. Choose the kindest response below each one.

- It's the first day of school, and you're excited to see all your old friends again. But then you notice a new girl who doesn't know anybody. You:

    A. Keep talking with your friends, figuring somebody else will talk to the new girl eventually.
    B. Think about how lonely and scared she must feel and invite her into your group of friends.

- Your teammate just missed the goal—for the second time—and you are really frustrated. You:

    A. Yell at her, saying, "What's your problem?"
    B. Realize she is frustrated too. Instead of yelling, you pat her on the back and say, "Shake it off."

- Dad grilled steaks for the family, but he overcooked them, and they are a bit burned. You:

    A. Let your dad know that the steaks are terrible.
    B. Thank your dad for taking time to cook.

Prayer Pointer

Jesus, help me notice the needs of others so
I can show them kindness like You do.

God did not give us a spirit that
makes us afraid. He gave us a spirit of
power and love and self-control.

2 Timothy 1:7

Have you ever felt so fidgety you thought you might fall out of your seat? Maybe you were sitting in class or at church for too long, or you were visiting with relatives while desperately wanting to go outside and play instead. Sometimes it feels like our bodies are in charge and telling us what to do. Instead of sitting and listening, we feel like running around and talking. Instead of working, we feel like playing or sleeping or eating. So which side of you wins?

If you are listening to God's Spirit, the self-controlled side will win. Self-control is exactly what it sounds like: controlling your mind and body to make them obedient to God. Even if you have off-the-chart ADHD, God can still help you tell your mind and body what it needs to be doing by His grace.

Why does it even matter? Because as children and soldiers of God, we are in a lifelong battle against evil in the world and sin inside ourselves. In order to train ourselves to follow God instead of caving in to every thought or desire we have, we have to use God's power of self-control, starting in the small things so that we know how to stand strong when the bigger temptations roll around.

Look at the situations on the next page. The ones on the left-hand side show lack of self-control. On the right-hand side, you can find the self-controlled solution to the situation. Draw a line from the left to the better solution on the right.

1. Eating the entire batch of cookies.
2. Blurting out the answer in class.
3. Throwing trash on the ground.
4. Watching TV instead of doing homework.
5. Hitting the snooze button for the fifth time.
6. Yelling at the person who is irritating you.
7. Telling the secret you promised not to tell.
8. Playing on the computer instead of exercising.
9. Shoving your way to the front of the line.

1. Raising your hand before you speak.
2. Patiently waiting until it is your turn.
3. Begin working first, taking short breaks after finishing each subject.
4. Putting two cookies on a plate and covering up the rest.
5. Keeping your mouth shut about the secret you're keeping.
6. Carving out time to play outside or exercise.
7. Praying for energy and direction, then getting out of bed to start your day.
8. Taking the time to put trash in the trash can.
9. Praying silently for wisdom and love, then talking respectfully to the irritating person.

Prayer Pointer

Lord, sometimes it's so difficult to control my thoughts and actions. Send Your Spirit to give me wisdom and strength to do the right thing.

I always pray to the God of our Lord Jesus
Christ . . . that He will give you a spirit that
will make you wise in the knowledge of God.

Ephesians 1:17

Consider this scenario:

Emily was one of the smartest girls in class. Without even studying, she could make straight As. But at home, Emily wasn't feeling so smart. Her parents had been fighting a lot, and she was worried, but she didn't know what to do. Should she talk to them about it, or would it be better to stay quiet? Could she trust her friend with this information, or would her friend gossip behind her back? Nothing in her school books could help Emily solve this real-life problem.

What would you say Emily needs to do in this situation?

_____

Why do you think that?

_____

Emily could sit there and think for hours or ask a bunch of different people their opinions on the situation, but how will she ever know which way is right? On her own, she can't. Emily needs wisdom in this situation, but she doesn't have it. Wisdom is far different from intelligence. Wisdom is the ability to understand life from God's perspective and to know and follow His directions.

Where do we get wisdom? From the wisest One in the universe,

of course! God says that if we will simply ask Him for wisdom, He will gladly give it to us. Sometimes He uses the Bible to give us the wisdom we are looking for. Sometimes He guides us through trusted parents or leaders who know His ways. Sometimes He simply works out the situation so that we see His power and control. However He chooses to do it, God is faithful to give us the wisdom of heaven to help us here with everything that happens on earth.

Look up these verses on wisdom, and record what you discover about wisdom in your own Prayer Pointer underneath, asking God to give you His kind of wisdom.

- James 1:5
- 2 Chronicles 1:11–12 (read the whole chapter about Solomon to get the bigger picture)
- Job 12:13
- Psalm 37:30
- Psalm 104:24
- Psalm 111:10
- 1 Corinthians 3:19
- James 3:17

Prayer Pointer

In all the work you are doing, work
the best you can. Work as if you were
working for the Lord, not for men.

Colossians 3:23

Paul's job to spread the gospel around the world wasn't an easy one. Everywhere he went, he met people eager to hear the Good News along with people who hated him for telling it and who wanted him to die. Some of the places were not easy to reach, requiring long boat trips in bad weather. Sometimes Paul was arrested, beaten, stoned, or rejected for what he had to say about Jesus. But Paul persevered—meaning he kept on going and working, even when it was difficult. In some of the towns, Paul also labored as a tentmaker so he could make money to live while sharing the gospel.

To put it mildly, Paul was a hard worker for Jesus. He knew that if he persevered in what he was doing, God would use his efforts to build the kingdom. What about you? When you are asked by your parents or teachers to do work that is difficult, what kind of attitude do you have? Do you give the work all of your attention and effort like Paul did, using all your energy to finish the task to the best of your ability? Or do you find ways to get around the work, stop in the middle, or fail to complete the task? Look at these scenarios on the next page. Mark an X through the ones showing laziness or other wrong attitudes. Circle the examples of perseverance and hard work.

1. Lindsey's mom asked her to clean up her room. Lindsey had other things to do, so she scooped all the clothes on her floor and stuffed them in her closet, where they couldn't be seen.
2. Allison's chore for the day was cleaning her room. First, she sorted all the things she found on the floor and counters. Then she put them all away in the right place until the room was clean.
3. Trysten missed more than half of the math problems on her homework last night. The teacher told her she could get more points if she reworked the ones she missed. But Trysten hates math and chose to watch TV instead.
4. Julia had the same problem with her math homework. Determined to do better, she asked her parents to show her what she was doing wrong. Then she reworked the problems until she understood how to do it.

—— PRAYER POINTER ——

Father, help me work hard, fight my own laziness, and finish the work You have asked me to do.

Never stop praying.

1 Thessalonians 5:17

When do you like to pray? Do you find it difficult or easy to do? Like most anything else, prayer becomes more natural to us the more we do it. In the beginning, though, when you are first learning how to talk to God, it can seem weird or scary. But just think, you are talking to the God of the universe—and He's listening to you! More amazing still, His Spirit, who lives inside you, will use God's Word to answer you back, keeping the conversation going from the time you wake up until your eyes close in sleep. And that's exactly what God wants: to share every part of your day with you, guiding, encouraging, talking, and listening as you learn to walk with your unseen best Friend. Here are some practical ways to get that conversation with God going:

1. Before you get out of bed in the morning, take a minute to say "Hi" or "Good morning" to God. Thank Him for being with you all the time.
2. Choose a certain time during the day specifically for prayer. You can start off with just five minutes. Then, as you grow stronger in your prayer life, lengthen the time. Don't let anything crowd out that time you have set apart for God.
3. Try praying out loud. After all, God loves to hear the praises of His people. Find a place where you won't be afraid of other people hearing you, and talk to God like He is standing right beside you—because He is! You just can't see Him.

4. Write down prayer reminders, and stick them places like the bathroom mirror or refrigerator to help you remember to talk to God.

5. Mealtimes are a common time to pray. But don't get stuck in the routine. Let your mind think about how much God provides for you, and give Him thanks from your heart.

6. Anytime you feel thankful about something, give thanks to God. All good gifts come from Him, even if it looks like it's coming from somewhere else.

7. Are you excited about something? Sad? Confused? Bored? Talk to God about it. In fact, talk to Him about everything. He cares, and He always knows how to direct your feet and mind to the right place.

Prayer Pointer

Lord Jesus, help me pray without stopping. I want to be as close to You as possible.

Order Up

All of you must obey the government
rulers. No one rules unless God has
given Him the power to rule. And no one
rules without that power from God.

Romans 13:1

I magine for a minute a large army led by captains and a general. Every soldier has a job and answers to the man in charge of him. And everything works like clockwork. Now imagine one day the men decide they are tired of doing what they are told. They get up when they feel like it. They argue when they're given orders. And they refuse to go through training.

What do you think would happen to that army when it went off to fight an enemy? Could an army like that even stay together?

A sense of order, with leaders and those being led, is absolutely necessary for armies to pull together and operate well. And the same is true for governments, cities, schools, and even families. Even though you may not like being told by your parents or teachers what to do, your obedience—even in the little things—is big-time important. When you obey your leaders, you are telling God that you trust the way He is leading you through the people He has put over you. Not only will you reap the benefits of staying safe and growing strong, but the whole group of people around you will function better as well. Look at the scenarios on the next page and write an *O* beside the examples of obedience and a *D* beside the ones that show disobedience.

_____ Riley's mom told everyone to turn off their electronic games at 8:00 p.m. Riley, however, was in the middle of the game and figured a few more minutes of playing wouldn't hurt anything.

_____ Casey had something important to tell her dad, but he was on the phone, and he motioned for her to wait. She stood quietly beside him until he was finished, and then she told him.

_____ "No talking in the hall," the teacher instructed the class as they were leaving for art. But she was up at the front of the line, so she never heard Bella and Lexi whispering in the back.

_____ "Would you please help me take all the groceries in?" Madeline's mom asked. Madeline went out to the car and brought in one bag and then went to her room.

PRAyeR PoiNteR

Jesus, help me obey my parents and leaders because I know it pleases You.

Understanding Honor

PRaise tHe LORD, all you wHo woRsHip Him. All
you descendants of Jacob, HONOR Him.

Psalm 22:23

The Israelites understood they needed to honor God when they witnessed Him on the mountain. If they hadn't figured it out from all the plagues God sent on the Egyptians, they could see it now: God was bigger, stronger, and holier than anything they could have imagined, and He deserved their full respect (Exodus 20).

When we show respect to the people in charge of us by following their directions, allowing them to speak while we listen, and recognizing their position of power over us, we are demonstrating the humble and obedient heart that God wants us to have. Look at the scenarios below, and mark an *R* on the ones that show respect. Write a *D* beside the ones that show disrespect.

- Ashley knew what her mom was going to say, so she interrupted her mom to tell her that she already knew.
- Some of the kids at school were taking God's name in vain. Eva asked politely if they would choose other words that didn't hurt God's name.
- "May I please go get some water?" Adrian asked after the teacher called on her.

PRayeR PoiNteR

Father, You are awesome and worthy of all my respect.
Help me show it to You and others with the way I live.

It Depends

We live in Him. We walk in Him. We are in Him.

Acts 17:28

You've probably said it a million times to your parents as you've gotten older: "I can do this myself!" For whatever reason, all of us want to show our family and friends that we are growing up and getting better at doing life. We feel proud about ourselves when we are able to do it on our own.

And that's natural. But growing up as a Christian is exactly the opposite experience. God wants us to learn more and more each day how much we *do* need Him. We can't do anything that matters on our own. The Bible even says that apart from God, we can do nothing. We are completely dependent on God for everything—and that's a beautiful thing. God is excited to help us and show us just how much He is able to do for us in our lives.

What do you need to depend on God for? We've started a brainstorming list. Can you add some other ways too?

- The air we breathe
- Our lives
- Growing faith
- Fighting our sin
- The clothes we wear
- Knowing what to pray
- Loving others well
- Getting along with family
- Understanding truth
- The food we eat

Prayer Pointer

Lord, I'm so excited about getting older and getting to do new, exciting things. Help me to always remember these opportunities and blessings come from You.

WHICH ONE of THESE CHARACTER TRAITS do you HAVE dowN pat? WHICH ONE could you use a little moRE bRushiNG up oN?

_____

_____

_____

_____

_____

_____

_____

_____

_____

_____

MIND GAMES

> "All people will know that you are my
> followers if you love each other."
>
> JOHN 13:35

Sometimes we have misperceptions about others in church and ourselves that can keep us from feeling comfortable with God's people and hinder our growth with God and others. Look at the list of misperceptions and wrong ideas below. Draw a line from each one to the truth on the right side that frees us to love God, ourselves, and others.

- They are more spiritual than I am.
- They already have friends and won't include me.
- They have more money and dress better than I do.
- I have nothing in common with these people.
- They seem perfect. I have a lot more problems.
- The teacher likes the others better.
- I sin too much to be here.
- I would be better off staying in bed.

- God rewards me when I seek Him. (Hebrews 11:6)
- Jesus is my forever Friend. I can risk reaching out to others because God is always with me. (Deuteronomy 31:6)
- The outside doesn't impress God. He values my heart. (1 Samuel 16:7)
- We are all sinners who desperately need Jesus. (Romans 3:23)
- Even though we're very different, we share the love of Jesus. (Colossians 3:11)
- Jesus always welcomes me. I am the apple of God's eye. (Matthew 19:14; Psalm 17:8)
- Jesus came to save sinners like me, not people who pretend to be righteous. (Luke 5:32)
- No one is righteous. We all suffer from sadness and sin in different ways. (Romans 3:9–10)

Prayer Pointer

God, thank You for always being my safe place
to land. Please help me to remember how
much You love me and help me each day.

The Name Game

He says, "Don't be afraid, because I have
saved you. I have called you by name, and
you are mine. . . . You are precious to
me. I give you honor, and I love you."

Isaiah 43:1, 4

Have you ever played the headband game? If not, grab a friend or a family member, and try this game on for laughs. The directions are for two people, but you can have as many pairs as you want!

What You Need:

- Stretchy headbands, one for each player
- 3 x 5-inch notecards
- A timer

Directions:

Write the names of as many objects, animals, or famous people you can think of on index cards, one item on each card. Shuffle the cards, and place the pile in the center with words facing down. Have each person put a headband around her forehead. Decide who is going to guess first, and place a card inside that person's headband without that person seeing the word on the card. Set the timer for three minutes. The one who can see the card tries to describe the word without actually saying the word. The other person tries to guess who or what is on the card based on the clues the other person

gives. If she guesses correctly, she grabs another one and repeats the process. After three minutes, tally how many answers the person guessed right. Then repeat the whole process, allowing the other partner to guess. The person at the end with the most cards wins!

The headband game is a ton of fun and promises to have everyone frantic and laughing at the end. But the name game in real life is not nearly as fun. Just like in the game, we often look around at everyone else, hoping they will tell us who we are (just without the cards on our heads). Are we funny? Pretty? Athletic? Exciting? Or are we weird? Ugly? Dumb? Unimportant? Sadly, we judge ourselves based on how everybody else seems to rate us. But God says to look up to the One who made you! Only God knows who you really are and who He has made you to be. Instead of letting other people name you, look in God's Word to see your true worth. Your value is greater than anything anyone could guess!

Prayer Pointer

God, You are the One who truly defines me.
Help me to always remember to look to
You for my worth and not the world.

You belong to the LORD your God. He
has chosen you from all the people
on earth to be His very own.

Deuteronomy 14:2

We all want to know what we're worth, and we hope it's enough. But we don't have to hope. We can know that we are priceless in God's eyes because of what He says in His Word. Read these passages, and then find these words in the word search that describe who you are in Jesus.

Prayer Pointer

Father, thank You for choosing me to be Your
daughter. Help me to find my worth in You.

New (Ephesians 2:10)   Forgiven (1 John 1:9)
Witness (Acts 1:8)   Friend (James 2:23; 1 John 3:2)
Chosen (Ephesians 1:4)   Temple (1 Corinthians 3:16)
Loved (2 Thessalonians 2:17) Child (John 1:12)
Soldier (2 Timothy 2:3)

```
T  H  L  C  N  L  G  F  R  C
F  E  C  G  O  V  O  P  M  H
N  W  M  V  C  R  R  E  K  I
F  K  E  P  G  B  N  R  R  L
X  D  B  I  L  E  F  J  E  D
P  R  V  S  S  E  N  T  I  W
W  E  N  O  J  A  J  N  D  X
N  M  H  F  Q  T  P  B  L  S
W  C  F  R  I  E  N  D  O  K
M  H  T  E  B  C  H  F  S  P
```

> God looked at everything He had
> made, and it was very good.
>
> Genesis 1:31

Did you know that God planned you before He even made the world? Yep, He knew exactly what color hair you'd have, what color eyes and skin, what personality. He had a purpose He created you for and chose the day you were born for a reason. You are no accident! Each part of you reflects God's creativity and glory. He thinks about you more than there are grains of sand in the sea! Read all of Psalm 139 to get the big picture. Then find the words that describe how God made us and sees us in the word search.

Prayer Pointer

Lord, I can be confident in who I am because You
love me and know me better than I know myself.

Known	Seen	Amazing
Surrounded	Made	Wonderful
Held	Formed	Planned

```
P  Z  A  H  W  V  U  L  M  C
B  L  O  W  X  R  F  U  W  B
N  O  A  K  N  L  O  F  M  T
D  E  D  N  U  O  R  R  U  S
R  D  E  V  N  D  M  E  P  U
U  A  O  S  Q  E  E  D  C  K
R  M  P  U  I  N  D  N  N  V
A  M  A  Z  I  N  G  O  U  J
D  L  E  H  O  P  W  W  H  Q
O  F  Y  L  W  N  K  B  L  L
```

Sheltered Sheep

We are His people, the sheep He tends.

Psalm 100:3

What keeps a sheep safe and sound? The shepherd, of course. And Jesus lets us know that we are His sheep, and He is the best Shepherd ever. Look up Psalm 23 and fill in the blanks below, including any worries or thoughts you have on your mind today that Jesus, your Shepherd, can handle.

The Lord is my _____.

    I have _____ I need (*including my food, my clothes, my

    _____, _____, _____,

    and _____).

He gives me _____ in green pastures.

    He leads me to calm _____.

He gives me new _____ (to do the following

    things: _____, _____, _____,

    _____, and even _____).

For the good of His name,

    He _____ me on paths that are _____.

Even if I _____

    through a very dark _____ (such as _____

    or _____), I *will not* be _____

    because (choose the right answer below)

    a. I am a tough kid.

    b. My parents will take care of me.

    c. God is with me.

Your _____ and your shepherd's staff _____ me.
You prepare a _____ for me
   in front of my enemies.
You pour _____ on my head (not to make it greasy, but to
  let me know I am a child of the King).
You give me _____ than I can hold.
Surely your _____ and _____will be
  with me _____ my life.
And I will _____ in the house of the _____forever!

PRayeR PoinTeR

**God, thank You for being my Good Shepherd. Help
me to be a loyal and faithful follower of You.**

> You can be sure that I will
> be with you always.
>
> Matthew 28:20

Have you ever noticed how much things—and even people—change over time? Friends come and go; we move to new places, change grades, and we even grow older. But God is the only One in our lives who *never* changes. He will stay just as loving and kind and good tomorrow as He is today. Best of all, He promises that *nothing* in this world can ever separate us from His love. No matter what we do or how our lives change, God will always love us. Read Romans 8:38–39. Then write your name in the center of the circle, beneath the name of Jesus. Outside the circle, write all of the things listed in Romans that God says can't come between you and Him. You are together forever!

Prayer Pointer

Thank You, God, for Your perfect love,
and that You will never leave me.

_____   _____   _____

_____   _____

JESUS

_____

_____   _____

_____

death • life • angels • ruling spirits
today's problems • the future • powers
forces above us • forces below us
anything in the whole world

We captuRe eveRy tHougHt and make
it give up and obey CHRist.

2 CoRiNtHiaNs 10:5

In the picture grid to the right, you will find two different kinds of thoughts: right ones and wrong ones. Sometimes we listen to the voice inside our heads that tells us the wrong message about ourselves and it makes us feel sad and ashamed. But God's Spirit inside us shouts the truth, that we are His beloved children. God tells us to shut out the lies and listen to His truth. Listen to God's voice telling you how His love turns away every bad thought.

Directions: use a dark crayon or marker to strike through the bad thoughts. Color the true statements pink. What does God want you to know about yourself? You are loved!

PRayeR PoiNteR

God, help me to listen to only the good thoughts in my
head because You tell me they speak Your truth.

I am dearly loved.

I'll never change.

I am a member of God's family.

No one loves me.

My sister/brother is better than me.

I can do all things through Christ.

I'm not good at anything.

I'm too bad to be forgiven.

God has given me every good thing I need.

Teachers don't like me.

No one has problems like me.

I'm unlovable.

I am wonderfully made.

I'm fat.

I am forgiven.

My parents enjoy me.

My teachers are God's gift to help me.

I am chosen by God.

No one wants to be my friend.

I have a special purpose.

Everyone else is prettier than me.

My parents don't like me.

I bring the fragrance of Jesus to the world.

I'm not smart.

Nothing can ever separate me from God's love.

You should do good deeds to be an example in every way.

Titus 2:7

Did you know that your parents aren't the only ones who have a job? You do too! You might not receive a paycheck as a reward, but the character benefits of helping your family are priceless. But how good of a helper are you? Take this quiz to find out.

1. Your mom just pulled into the driveway with a car full of groceries. You:
    A. Take your game to your room where your mom won't find you.
    B. Wait until she brings everything in so you can find the food you wanted.
    C. Carry a couple of bags in just so you can say you helped.
    D. Help carry all the bags inside and help her put away the items.

2. Your dad is talking with a client on the phone at home. You:
    A. Turn up the TV louder so that you can hear it over your dad.
    B. Keep running, laughing, and playing in the same room even after he motions for you to be quiet.
    C. Keep tugging on his sleeve to get his attention because you want something.
    D. Get your brothers and sisters to quietly leave the room so he can finish his business in peace.

3. Your sister is struggling with her math, which happens to be your best subject. You:
    A. Make fun of her for not understanding anything.
    B. Tell her she's on her own because you have homework of your own.
    C. Get frustrated with her because she didn't understand right away when you explained it.
    D. Patiently show her how to do the problem until she gets it; then praise her when she does.

4. Your aging relatives want you and your family to visit. You:
    A. Tell your mom you want to go to a friend's house instead.
    B. Roll your eyes and moan.
    C. Go, but you play on your electronic device the whole time.
    D. Go, hug them, listen, and answer their questions while looking them in the eye.

If you answered *D* for every question, congratulations! You're an expert family helper and a very important part of your family's support system. If you answered *A*, *B*, or *C* for any of the above, ask yourself, "Who am I serving in this situation?" Then ask God to help you become a better helper for your family.

PRayeR PoiNteR

Thank You for my family, God. Help me
to be a better helper for them.

Do the best you can to be the kind of person that God will approve, and give yourself to Him. Be a worker who is not ashamed of his work—a worker who uses the true teaching in the right way.

2 Timothy 2:15

E verybody has to go to school. But not everybody has a good attitude about it. Whether or not we always score *As* on the report card, we are told to do our very best. But *why*? Because God says we should love Him with all of our minds, as well as our hearts, souls, and strength. Even when we're studying math, science, English, or history, we are still learning about how God made this world and has power over it. Everything points to Him, so we should concentrate on learning—and living—this truth as much as we can. How are your study habits? Take this quiz and check your score at the end.

1. You are supposed to read a lengthy book for English, but it is very difficult. You:
    A. Read it anyway, and go online, to your parents, and to your teacher for help.
    B. Read the first chapter and then give up. You can make up the grade other places.
    C. Never open the book. Ask your friends to tell you the story instead.

2. You are ready for school and have a few minutes to spare before leaving. You:
    A. Spend some time in the Bible and prayer.

B. Get irritated that you have to wait on everybody else to ge~
ready.

C. Play on your video game.

3. The teacher assigned a project that is due two weeks from today. You:

A. Figure out what needs to be done and start on it within the week.

B. Relax because nobody else is working on it either.

C. Wait until the night before the project is due to start working on it.

4. When it comes to memorizing God's Word, you:

A. Make it a priority, working on different verses each week.

B. Figure you can always look verses up on the Internet if you need it.

C. Never even think about it.

5. You work hard on your schoolwork because:

A. You know it honors God, and you want it to help you be the person God made you to be.

B. Good grades make you look really smart and the teachers like you more.

C. You are very competitive and want to beat the other kids.

If you answered *A* in the above questions, you get an *A* for applying yourself well in your study work, honoring God as you grow! Answers *B* or *C* reveal your tendency to wait until the last minute, along with some laziness, which keeps you from being able to do your best. Ask God to help you care about His Word and the world He has made by doing your very best in your studies—all for His glory.

Prayer Pointer

God, I want to honor You by working hard
to be the best person I can be.

Whoever does not love does not
know God, because God is love.

1 John 4:8

You may have heard that God loves you, but what does *love* really mean? Look at the passage of 1 Corinthians 13:4–8 below. It has been printed out three times to give you a new look at love. The first passage shows what love is, as recorded in 1 Corinthians.

> Love is patient and kind. Love is not jealous, it does not brag, and it is not proud. Love is not rude, is not selfish, and does not become angry easily. Love does not remember wrongs done against it. Love is not happy with evil, but is happy with the truth. Love patiently accepts all things. It always trusts, always hopes, and always continues strong. Love never ends.

Next, think about the fact that God *is* love. That means everything written about love in this passage reflects how God is. In each blank, fill in the name Jesus or God. Then read the passage again with God's name in front.

_____ is patient and kind. _____ is not jealous, _____ does not brag, and _____ is not proud. _____ is not rude, _____ is not selfish, and does not become angry easily. _____ does not remember

wrongs done against [Him]. _____ is not happy with evil, but is happy with the truth. _____ patiently accepts all things. _____ always trusts, always hopes, and always continues strong. _____ never ends.

In this last exercise, try putting your own name in the blanks where *love* should go. Do you think it is a good representation of how you actually act? All of us need to grow in love to become like God, our Father. Why not ask Him now to help you love like Him?

_____ is patient and kind. _____ is not jealous, _____ does not brag, and _____ is not proud. _____ is not rude, _____ is not selfish, and does not become angry easily. _____ does not remember wrongs done against [her]. _____ is not happy with evil, but is happy with the truth. _____ patiently accepts all things. _____ always trusts, always hopes, and always continues strong. _____ never ends.

—— Prayer Pointer ——

Jesus, thank You for always loving me. Help
me love You and others in the same way.

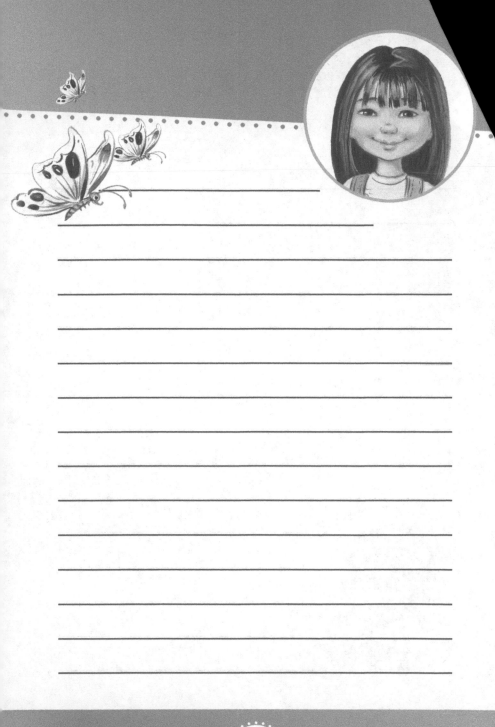

Notes